A.B. "BANJO"

Paterson

A Book of Verse

For Sr. Maryanna,

   A little of Australia
for the much enjoyment you
have given me.
   Your brother in Our Holy Father Dominic
      Anthony Walsh O.P.

ANGUS
& ROBERTSON

AN ANGUS & ROBERTSON BOOK

First published in Australia in 1990 by
Collins/Angus & Robertson Publishers Australia

Collins/Angus & Robertson Publishers Australia
Unit 4, Eden Park, 31 Waterloo Road, North Ryde
NSW 2113, Australia

William Collins Publishers Ltd
31 View Road, Glenfield, Auckland 10, New Zealand

Angus & Robertson (UK)
16 Golden Square, London W1R 4BN, United Kingdom

Copyright © Retusa Pty Ltd 1990

National Library of Australia
Cataloguing-in-Publication data:

Paterson, A. B. (Andrew Barton) 1864–1941.
  A. B. Paterson, a book of verse.
  Includes index.
  ISBN 0 207 16862 8.
  I. Title.
A821.2

Typeset in Century Old Style by Savage Type, Australia
Printed in Singapore

5 4 3 2 1
95 94 93 92 91 90

Contents

A Singer of the Bush

There is waving of grass in the breeze
    And a song in the air,
And a murmur of myriad bees
    That toil everywhere.
There is scent in the blossom and bough,
    And the breath of the spring
Is as soft as a kiss on a brow —
    And springtime I sing.

There is drought on the land, and the stock
    Tumble down in their tracks
Or follow — a tottering flock —
    The scrub-cutter's axe.
While ever a creature survives
    The axes shall swing;
We are fighting with fate for their lives —
    And the combat I sing.

Over the Range

Little bush maiden, wondering-eyed,
    Playing alone in the creek bed dry,
In the small green flat on every side
    Walled in by the Moonbi Ranges high;
Tell us the tale of your lonely life,
    'Mid the great grey forests that know no change.
"I never have left my home," she said,
    "I have never been over the Moonbi Range.

"Father and mother are both long dead,
    And I live with granny in yon wee place."
"Where are your father and mother?" we said.
    She puzzled awhile with thoughtful face,
Then a light came into the shy brown eye,
    And she smiled, for she thought the question strange
On a thing so certain — "When people die
    They go to the country over the range."

"And what is this country like, my lass?"
    "There are blossoming trees and pretty flowers,
And shining creeks where the golden grass
    Is fresh and sweet from the summer showers.
They never need work, nor want, nor weep;
    No troubles can come their hearts to estrange.
Some summer night I shall fall asleep,
    And wake in the country over the range."

Child, you are wise in your simple trust,
    For the wisest man knows no more than you.
Ashes to ashes, and dust to dust:
    Our views by a range are bounded too;

But we know that God hath this gift in store,
That when we come to the final change,
We shall meet with our loved ones gone before
To the beautiful country over the range.

Lost

"He ought to be home," said the old man, "without there's
  something amiss.
He only went to the Two-mile — he ought to be back by this.
He *would* ride the Reckless filly, he *would* have his wilful way;
And, here, he's not back at sundown — and what will his mother say?

"He was always his mother's idol, since ever his father died;
And there isn't a horse on the station that he isn't game to ride.
But that Reckless mare is vicious, and if once she gets away
He hasn't got strength to hold her — and what will his mother say?"

The old man walked to the sliprail, and peered up the dark'ning track,
And looked and longed for the rider that would never more come back;
And the mother came and clutched him, with sudden, spasmodic fright:
"What has become of my Willie? Why isn't he home tonight?"

Away in the gloomy ranges, at the foot of an ironbark,
The bonnie, winsome laddie was lying stiff and stark;
For the Reckless mare had smashed him against a leaning limb,
And his comely face was battered, and his merry eyes were dim.

And the thoroughbred chestnut filly, the saddle beneath her flanks,
Was away like fire through the ranges to join the wild mob's ranks;

And a broken-hearted woman and an old man worn and grey
Were searching all night in the ranges till the sunrise brought the day.

And the mother kept feebly calling, with a hope that would not die,
"Willie! where are you, Willie?" But how can the dead reply;
And hope died out with the daylight, and the darkness brought despair,
God pity the stricken mother, and answer the widow's prayer!

Though far and wide they sought him, they found not where he fell;
For the ranges held him precious, and guarded their treasure well.
The wattle blooms above him, and the bluebells blow close by,
And the brown bees buzz the secret, and the wild birds sing reply.

But the mother pined and faded, and cried, and took no rest,
And rode each day to the ranges on her hopeless, weary quest.
Seeking her loved one ever, she faded and pined away,
But with strength of her great affection she still sought every day.

"I know that sooner or later I shall find my boy," she said.
But she came not home one evening, and they found her lying dead,
And stamped on the poor pale features, as the spirit homeward pass'd,
Was an angel smile of gladness — she had found the boy at last.

Clancy of The Overflow

I had written him a letter which I had, for want of better
    Knowledge, sent to where I met him down the Lachlan, years ago;
He was shearing when I knew him, so I sent the letter to him,
    Just "on spec", addressed as follows: "Clancy, of The Overflow".

And an answer came directed in a writing unexpected,
    (And I think the same was written with a thumbnail dipped in tar);
'Twas his shearing mate who wrote it, and *verbatim* I will quote it:
    "Clancy's gone to Queensland droving, and we don't know
        where he are."

*   *   *   *

In my wild erratic fancy visions come to me of Clancy
    Gone a-droving "down the Cooper" where the Western drovers go;
As the stock are slowly stringing, Clancy rides behind them singing,
    For the drover's life has pleasures that the townsfolk never know.

And the bush hath friends to meet him, and their kindly voices greet him
    In the murmur of the breezes and the river on its bars,
And he sees the vision splendid of the sunlit plains extended,
    And at night the wondrous glory of the everlasting stars.

*   *   *   *

I am sitting in my dingy little office, where a stingy
    Ray of sunlight struggles feebly down between the houses tall,
And the foetid air and gritty of the dusty, dirty city
    Through the open window floating, spreads its foulness over all.

And in place of lowing cattle, I can hear the fiendish rattle
    Of the tramways and the buses making hurry down the street,
And the language uninviting of the gutter children fighting
    Comes fitfully and faintly through the ceaseless tramp of feet.

And the hurrying people daunt me, and their pallid faces haunt me
　　As they shoulder one another in their rush and nervous haste,
With their eager eyes and greedy, and their stunted forms and weedy,
　　For townsfolk have no time to grow, they have no time to waste.

And I somehow rather fancy that I'd like to change with Clancy,
　　Like to take a turn at droving where the seasons come and go,
While he faced the round eternal of the cashbook and the journal —
　　But I doubt he'd suit the office, Clancy, of "The Overflow".

The Man from Snowy River

There was movement at the station, for the word had passed around
　　That the colt from old Regret had got away,
And had joined the wild bush horses — he was worth a thousand pound,
So all the cracks had gathered to the fray.
All the tried and noted riders from the stations near and far
Had mustered at the homestead overnight,
For the bushmen love hard riding where the wild bush horses are,
And the stock horse snuffs the battle with delight.

There was Harrison, who made his pile when Pardon won the cup,
The old man with his hair as white as snow;
But few could ride beside him when his blood was fairly up —
He would go wherever horse and man could go.
And Clancy of the Overflow came down to lend a hand,
No better horseman ever held the reins;

For never horse could throw him while the saddle girths would stand,
He learnt to ride while droving on the plains.

And one was there, a stripling on a small and weedy beast,
He was something like a racehorse undersized,
With a touch of Timor pony — three parts thoroughbred at least —
And such as are by mountain horsemen prized.
He was hard and tough and wiry — just the sort that won't say die —
There was courage in his quick impatient tread;
And he bore the badge of gameness in his bright and fiery eye,
And the proud and lofty carriage of his head.

But still so slight and weedy, one would doubt his power to stay,
And the old man said, "That horse will never do
For a long and tiring gallop — lad, you'd better stop away,
Those hills are far too rough for such as you."
So he waited sad and wistful — only Clancy stood his friend —
"I think we ought to let him come," he said;
"I warrant he'll be with us when he's wanted at the end,
For both his horse and he are mountain bred.

"He hails from Snowy River, up by Kosciusko's side,
Where the hills are twice as steep and twice as rough,
Where a horse's hoofs strike firelight from the flint stones every stride,
The man that holds his own is good enough.
And the Snowy River riders on the mountains make their home,
Where the river runs those giant hills between;
I have seen full many horsemen since I first commenced to roam,
But nowhere yet such horsemen have I seen."

So he went — they found the horses by the big mimosa clump —
They raced away towards the mountain's brow,
And the old man gave his orders, "Boys, go at them from the jump,
No use to try for fancy riding now.
And, Clancy, you must wheel them, try and wheel them to the right.

7

Ride boldly, lad, and never fear the spills,
For never yet was rider that could keep the mob in sight,
If once they gain the shelter of those hills."

So Clancy rode to wheel them — he was racing on the wing
Where the best and boldest riders take their place,
And he raced his stockhorse past them, and he made the ranges ring
With the stockwhip, as he met them face to face.
Then they halted for a moment, while he swung the dreaded lash,
But they saw their well-loved mountain full in view,
And they charged beneath the stockwhip with a sharp and sudden dash,
And off into the mountain scrub they flew.

Then fast the horsemen followed, where the gorges deep and black
Resounded to the thunder of their tread,
And the stockwhips woke the echoes, and they fiercely answered back
From cliffs and crags that beetled overhead.
And upward, ever upward, the wild horses held their way,
Where mountain ash and kurrajong grew wide;
And the old man muttered fiercely, "We may bid the mob good day,
No man can hold them down the other side."

When they reached the mountain's summit, even Clancy took a pull,
It well might make the boldest hold their breath,
The wild hop scrub grew thickly, and the hidden ground was full
Of wombat holes, and any slip was death.
But the man from Snowy River let the pony have his head,
And he swung his stockwhip round and gave a cheer,
And he raced him down the mountain like a torrent down its bed,
While the others stood and watched in very fear.

He sent the flint stones flying, but the pony kept his feet,
He cleared the fallen timber in his stride,
And the man from Snowy River never shifted in his seat —
It was grand to see that mountain horseman ride.

Through the stringybarks and saplings, on the rough and broken ground,
Down the hillside at a racing pace he went;
And he never drew the bridle till he landed safe and sound,
At the bottom of that terrible descent.

He was right among the horses as they climbed the further hill,
And the watchers on the mountain standing mute,
Saw him ply the stockwhip fiercely, he was right among them still,
As he raced across the clearing in pursuit.
Then they lost him for a moment, where two mountain gullies met
In the ranges, but a final glimpse reveals
On a dim and distant hillside the wild horses racing yet,
With the man from Snowy River at their heels.

And he ran them single-handed till their sides were white with foam.
He followed like a bloodhound on their track,
Till they halted cowed and beaten, then he turned their heads for home,
And alone and unassisted brought them back.
But his hardy mountain pony he could scarcely raise a trot,
He was blood from hip to shoulder from the spur;
But his pluck was still undaunted, and his courage fiery hot,
For never yet was mountain horse a cur.

And down by Kosciusko, where the pine-clad ridges raise
Their torn and rugged battlements on high,
Where the air is clear as crystal, and the white stars fairly blaze
At midnight in the cold and frosty sky,
And where around The Overflow the reed beds sweep and sway
To the breezes, and the rolling plains are wide,
The man from Snowy River is a household word today,
And the stockmen tell the story of his ride.

Those Names

The shearers sat in the firelight, hearty and hale and strong,
After the hard day's shearing, passing the joke along:
The "ringer" that shore a hundred, as they never were shorn before,
And the novice who, toiling bravely, had tommyhawked half a score,
The tar boy, the cook, and the slushy, the sweeper that swept the board,
The picker-up, and the penner, with the rest of the shearing horde.
There were men from the inland stations where the skies
    like a furnace glow,
And men from the Snowy River, the land of the frozen snow;
There were swarthy Queensland drovers who reckoned all land by miles,
And farmers' sons from the Murray, where many a vineyard smiles.
They started at telling stories when they wearied of cards and games,
And to give these stories a flavour they threw in some local names,
And a man from the bleak Monaro, away on the tableland,
He fixed his eyes on the ceiling, and he started to play his hand.

He told them of Adjintoothbong, where the pine-clad mountains freeze,
And the weight of the snow in summer breaks branches off the trees,
And, as he warmed to the business, he let them have it strong —
Nimitybelle, Conargo, Wheeo, Bongongolong;
He lingered over them fondly, because they recalled to mind
A thought of the old bush homestead, and the girl that he left behind.
Then the shearers all sat silent till a man in the corner rose;
Said he, "I've travelled aplenty but never heard names like those,
Out in the western districts, out on the Castlereagh
Most of the names are easy — short for a man to say.
You've heard of Mungrybambone and the Gundabluey pine,
Quobbotha, Girilambone, and Terramungamine,
Quambone, Eunonyhareenyha, Wee Waa, and Buntijo —"

10

But the rest of the shearers stopped him, "For the sake of your jaw,
   go slow,
If you reckon those names are short ones out where such names prevail,
Just try and remember some long ones before you begin the tale."

And the man from the western district, though never a word he said,
Just winked with his dexter eyelid, and then he retired to bed.

On Kiley's Run

The roving breezes come and go
   On Kiley's Run,
The sleepy river murmurs low,
And far away one dimly sees
Beyond the stretch of forest trees —
Beyond the foothills dusk and dun —
The ranges sleeping in the sun
   On Kiley's Run.

'Tis many years since first I came
   To Kiley's Run,
More years than I would care to name
Since I, a stripling, used to ride
For miles and miles at Kiley's side,
The while in stirring tones he told
The stories of the days of old
   On Kiley's Run.

11

I see the old bush homestead now
   On Kiley's Run,
Just nestled down beneath the brow
Of one small ridge above the sweep
Of river flat, where willows weep
And jasmine flowers and roses bloom,
The air was laden with perfume
   On Kiley's Run.

We lived the good old station life
   On Kiley's Run,
With little thought of care or strife.
Old Kiley seldom used to roam,
He liked to make the Run his home,
The swagman never turned away
With empty hand at close of day
   From Kiley's Run.

We kept a racehorse now and then
   On Kiley's Run,
And neighb'ring stations brought their men
To meetings where the sport was free,
And dainty ladies came to see
Their champions ride; with laugh and song
The old house rang the whole night long
   On Kiley's Run.

The station hands were friends I wot
   On Kiley's Run,
A reckless, merry-hearted lot —
All splendid riders, and they knew
The "boss" was kindness through and through.
Old Kiley always stood their friend,

And so they served him to the end
    On Kiley's Run.

But droughts and losses came apace
    To Kiley's Run,
Till ruin stared him in the face;
He toiled and toiled while lived the light,
He dreamed of overdrafts at night:
At length, because he could not pay,
His bankers took the stock away
    From Kiley's Run.

Old Kiley stood and saw them go
    From Kiley's Run.
The well-bred cattle marching slow;
His stockmen, mates for many a day,
They wrung his hand and went away.
Too old to make another start,
Old Kiley died — of broken heart,
    On Kiley's Run.

The owner lives in England now
    Of Kiley's Run.
He knows a racehorse from a cow;
But that is all he knows of stock:
His chiefest care is how to dock
Expenses, and he sends from town
To cut the shearers' wages down
    On Kiley's Run.

There are no neighbours anywhere
    Near Kiley's Run.
The hospitable homes are bare,
The gardens gone; for no pretence
Must hinder cutting down expense:

The homestead that we held so dear
Contains a half-paid overseer
    On Kiley's Run.

All life and sport and hope have died
    On Kiley's Run.
No longer there the stockmen ride;
For sour-faced boundary riders creep
On mongrel horses after sheep,
Through ranges where, at racing speed,
Old Kiley used to "wheel the lead"
    On Kiley's Run.

There runs a lane for thirty miles
    Through Kiley's Run.
On either side the herbage smiles,
But wretched trav'lling sheep must pass
Without a drink or blade of grass
Thro' that long lane of death and shame:
The weary drovers curse the name
    Of Kiley's Run.

The name itself is changed of late
    Of Kiley's Run.
They call it "Chandos Park Estate".
The lonely swagman through the dark
Must hump his swag past Chandos Park.
The name is English, don't you see,
The old name sweeter sounds to me
    Of "Kiley's Run".

I cannot guess what fate will bring
    To Kiley's Run —
For chances come and changes ring —
I scarcely think 'twill always be

Locked up to suit an absentee;
And if he lets it out in farms
His tenants soon will carry arms
   On Kiley's Run.

Come-by-Chance

As I pondered very weary o'er a volume long and dreary —
   For the plot was void of interest — 'twas that Postal Guide, in fact,
There I learnt the true location, distance, size, and population
Of each township, town, and village in the radius of the Act.

And I learnt that Puckawidgee stands beside the Murrumbidgee,
And that Booleroi and Bumble get their letters twice a year,
Also that the post inspector, when he visited Collector,
Closed the office up instanter, and re-opened Dungalear.

But my languid mood forsook me, when I found a name that took me,
Quite by chance I came across it — "Come-by-Chance" was what I read;
No location was assigned it, not a thing to help one find it,
Just an "N" which stood for northward, and the rest was all unsaid.

I shall leave my home, and forthward wander stoutly to the northward
Till I come by chance across it, and I'll straightway settle down,
For there can't be any hurry, nor the slightest cause for worry
Where the telegraph don't reach you nor the railways run to town.

And one's letters and exchanges come by chance across the ranges,
Where a wiry young Australian leads a pack horse once a week,

15

And the good news grows by keeping, and you're spared the pain
　　of weeping
Over bad news when the mailman drops the letters in the creek.

But I fear, and more's the pity, that there's really no such city,
For there's not a man can find it of the shrewdest folk I know,
"Come-by-Chance", be sure it never means a land of fierce endeavour,
It is just the careless country where the dreamers only go.

　　　　　　　*　　*　　*　　*

Though we work and toil and hustle in our life of haste and bustle,
All that makes our life worth living comes unstriven for and free;
Man may weary and importune, but the fickle goddess Fortune
Deals him out his pain or pleasure careless what his worth may be.

All the happy times entrancing, days of sport and nights of dancing,
Moonlit rides and stolen kisses, pouting lips and loving glance:
When you think of these be certain you have looked behind the curtain,
You have had the luck to linger just a while in "Come-by-Chance".

In the Droving Days

"Only a pound," said the auctioneer,
　　"Only a pound; and I'm standing here
Selling this animal, gain or loss.
Only a pound for the drover's horse;
One of the sort that was ne'er afraid,
One of the boys of the Old Brigade;
Thoroughly honest and game, I'll swear,

Only a little the worse for wear;
Plenty as bad to be seen in town,
Give me a bid and I'll knock him down;
Sold as he stands, and without recourse,
Give me a bid for the drover's horse."

Loitering there in an aimless way
Somehow I noticed the poor old grey,
Weary and battered and screwed, of course,
Yet when I noticed the old grey horse,
The rough bush saddle, and single rein
Of the bridle laid on his tangled mane,
Straightway the crowd and the auctioneer
Seemed on a sudden to disappear,
Melted away in a kind of haze,
For my heart went back to the droving days.

Back to the road, and I crossed again
Over the miles of the saltbush plain —
The shining plain that is said to be
The dried-up bed of an inland sea,
Where the air so dry and so clear and bright
Refracts the sun with a wondrous light,
And out in the dim horizon makes
The deep blue gleam of the phantom lakes.

At dawn of day we would feel the breeze
That stirred the boughs of the sleeping trees,
And brought a breath of the fragrance rare
That comes and goes in that scented air;
For the trees and grass and the shrubs contain
A dry sweet scent on the saltbush plain.
For those that love it and understand,
The saltbush plain is a wonderland.

A wondrous country, where nature's ways
Were revealed to me in the droving days.

We saw the fleet wild horses pass,
And the kangaroos through the Mitchell grass,
The emu ran with her frightened brood
All unmolested and unpursued.
But there rose a shout and a wild hubbub
When the dingo raced for his native scrub,
And he paid right dear for his stolen meals
With the drovers' dogs at his wretched heels.
For we ran him down at a rattling pace,
While the pack horse joined in the stirring chase.
And a wild halloo at the kill we'd raise —
We were light of heart in the droving days.

'Twas a drover's horse, and my hand again
Made a move to close on a fancied rein.
For I felt the swing and the easy stride
Of the grand old horse that I used to ride
In drought or plenty, in good or ill,
That same old steed was my comrade still;
The old grey horse with his honest ways
Was a mate to me in the droving days.

When we kept our watch in the cold and damp,
If the cattle broke from the sleeping camp,
Over the flats and across the plain,
With my head bent down on his waving mane,
Through the boughs above and the stumps below
On the darkest night I would let him go
At a racing speed; he would choose his course,
And my life was safe with the old grey horse.
But man and horse had a favourite job,

When an outlaw broke from a station mob,
With a right good will was the stockwhip plied,
As the old horse raced at the straggler's side,
And the greenhide whip such a weal would raise,
We could use the whip in the droving days.

*   *   *   *

"Only a pound!" and was this the end —
Only a pound for the drover's friend.
The drover's friend that had seen his day,
And now was worthless, and cast away
With a broken knee and a broken heart
To be flogged and starved in a hawker's cart.
Well, I made a bid for a sense of shame
And the memories dear of the good old game.

"Thank you? Guinea! and cheap at that!
Against you there in the curly hat!
Only a guinea, and one more chance,
Down he goes if there's no advance,
Third, and the last time, one! two! three!"
And the old grey horse was knocked down to me.
And now he's wandering, fat and sleek,
On the lucerne flats by the Homestead Creek;
I dare not ride him for fear he'd fall,
But he does a journey to beat them all,
For though he scarcely a trot can raise,
He can take me back to the droving days.

An Evening in Dandaloo

It was while we held our races —
    Hurdles, sprints and steeplechases —
  Up in Dandaloo,
That a crowd of Sydney stealers,
Jockeys, pugilists and spielers
Brought some horses, real heelers,
   Came and put us through.

Beat our nags and won our money,
Made the game by no means funny,
   Made us rather blue;
When the racing was concluded,
Of our hard-earned coin denuded
Dandaloonies sat and brooded
    There in Dandaloo.

        *   *   *   *

Night came down on Johnson's shanty
Where the grog was no means scanty,
   And a tumult grew
Till some wild, excited person
Galloped down the township cursing,
"Sydney push have mobbed Macpherson,
   Roll up, Dandaloo!"

Great St Denis! what commotion!
Like the rush of stormy ocean
   Fiery horsemen flew.
Dust and smoke and din and rattle,
Down the street they spurred their cattle
To the war-cry of the battle,
   "Wade in, Dandaloo!"

So the boys might have their fight out,
Johnson blew the bar-room light out,
   Then, in haste, withdrew.
And in darkness and in doubting
Raged the conflict and the shouting,
"Give the Sydney push a clouting,
   Go it, Dandaloo!"

Jack Macpherson seized a bucket,
Every head he saw, he struck it —
   Struck in earnest, too;
And a man from Lower Wattle,
Whom a shearer tried to throttle,
Hit out freely with a bottle,
   There in Dandaloo.

Skin and hair were flying thickly,
When a light was fetched, and quickly
   Brought a fact to view —
On the scene of the diversion
Every single, solid person
Came along to help Macpherson —
   All were Dandaloo!

When the list of slain was tabled,
Some were drunk and some disabled,
   Still we found it true.
In the darkness and the smother
We'd been belting one another;
Jack Macpherson bashed his brother
   There in Dandaloo.

So we drank, and all departed —
How the "mobbing" yarn was started
   No one ever knew —

And the stockmen tell the story
Of that conflict fierce and gory,
How we fought for love and glory
   Up in Dandaloo.

It's a proverb now, or near it —
At the races you can hear it,
   At the dog fights, too;
Every shrieking, dancing drover,
As the canines topple over,
Yells applause to Grip or Rover,
   "Give him 'Dandaloo'!"

And the teamster slowly toiling
Through the deep black country soiling
   Wheels and axles, too,
Lays the whip on Spot and Banker,
Rouses Tarboy with a flanker —
"Redman! Ginger! Heave there! Yank her!
   Wade in, Dandaloo!"

As Long As Your Eyes Are Blue

Wilt thou love me, sweet, when my hair is grey,
    And my cheeks shall have lost their hue?
When the charms of youth shall have passed away,
    Will your love as of old prove true?
For the looks may change, and the heart may range,
    And the love be no longer fond;
Wilt thou love with truth in the years of youth
    And away to the years beyond?

Oh, I love you, sweet, for your locks of brown
    And the blush on your cheek that lies —
But I love you most for the kindly heart
    That I see in your sweet blue eyes —
For the eyes are signs of the soul within,
    Of the heart that is leal and true,
And mine own sweetheart, I shall love you still,
    Just as long as your eyes are blue.

For the locks may bleach, and the cheeks of peach
    May be reft of their golden hue;
But mine own sweetheart, I shall love you still,
    Just as long as your eyes are blue.

Been There Before

There came a stranger to Walgett town,
  To Walgett town when the sun was low,
And he carried a thirst that was worth a crown,
  Yet how to quench it he did not know;
But he thought he might take those yokels down,
The guileless yokels of Walgett town.

They made him a bet in a private bar,
  In a private bar when the talk was high,
And they bet him some pounds no matter how far
  He could pelt a stone, yet he could not shy
A stone right over the river so brown,
The Darling River at Walgett town.

He knew that the river from bank to bank
  Was fifty yards, and he smiled a smile
As he trundled down, but his hopes they sank
  For there wasn't a stone within fifty mile;
For the saltbush plain and the open down
Produce no quarries in Walgett town.

The yokels laughed at his hopes o'erthrown,
  And he stood awhile like a man in a dream;
Then out of his pocket he fetched a stone,
  And pelted it over the silent stream —
He had been there before: he had wandered down
On a previous visit to Walgett town.

The Open Steeplechase

I had ridden over hurdles up the country once or twice,
  By the side of Snowy River with a horse they called "The Ace".
And we brought him down to Sydney, and our rider, Jimmy Rice,
Got a fall and broke his shoulder, so they nabbed me in a trice —
Me, that never wore the colours, for the Open Steeplechase.

"Make the running," said the trainer, "it's your only chance whatever,
Make it hot from start to finish, for the old black horse can stay,
And just think of how they'll take it, when they hear on Snowy River
That the country boy was plucky, and the country horse was clever.
You must ride for old Monaro and the mountain boys today."

"Are you ready?" said the starter, as we held the horses back,
All ablazing with impatience, with excitement all aglow;
Before us like a ribbon stretched the steeplechasing track,
And the sunrays glistened brightly on the chestnut and the black
As the starter's words came slowly, "Are — you — ready? Go!"

Well, I scarcely knew we'd started, I was stupid-like with wonder
Till the field closed up beside me and a jump appeared ahead.
And we flew it like a hurdle, not a baulk and not a blunder,
As we charged it all together, and it fairly whistled under,
And then some were pulled behind me and a few shot out and led.

So we ran for half the distance, and I'm making no pretences
When I tell you I was feeling very nervous-like and queer,
For those jockeys rode like demons; you would think they'd lost
    their senses
If you saw them rush their horses at those rasping five foot fences —
And in place of making running I was falling to the rear.

Till a chap came racing past me on a horse they called "The Quiver",
And said he, "My country joker, are you going to give it best?
Are you frightened of the fences? Does their stoutness make you shiver?
Have they come to breeding cowards by the side of Snowy River?
Are there riders on Monaro? —" but I never heard the rest.

For I drove The Ace and sent him just as fast as he could pace it,
At the big black line of timber stretching fair across the track,
And he shot beside The Quiver. "Now," said I, "my boy, we'll race it.
You can come with Snowy River if you're only game to face it;
Let us mend the pace a little and we'll see who cries a crack."

So we raced away together, and we left the others standing,
And the people cheered and shouted as we settled down to ride,
And we clung beside The Quiver. At his taking off and landing
I could see his scarlet nostril and his mighty ribs expanding,
And The Ace stretched out in earnest and we held him stride for stride.

But the pace was so terrific that they soon ran out their tether —
They were rolling in their gallop, they were fairly blown and beat —
But they both were game as pebbles — neither one would show
    the feather.
And we rushed them at the fences, and they cleared them both together,
Nearly every time they clouted but they somehow kept their feet.

Then the last jump rose before us, and they faced it game as ever —
We were both at spur and whipcord, fetching blood at every bound —
And above the people's cheering and the cries of "Ace" and "Quiver",
I could hear the trainer shouting, "One more run for Snowy River".
Then we struck the jump together and came smashing to the ground.

Well, The Quiver ran to blazes, but The Ace stood still and waited,
Stood and waited like a statue while I scrambled on his back.
There was no one next or near me for the field was fairly slated,
So I cantered home a winner with my shoulder dislocated,
While the man that rode The Quiver followed limping down the track.

And he shook my hand and told me that in all his days he never
Met a man who rode more gamely, and our last set to was prime,
And we wired them on Monaro how we chanced to beat The Quiver.
And they sent us back an answer, "Good old sort from Snowy River;
Send us word each race you start in and we'll back you every time."

In Defence of the Bush

So you're back from up the country, Mister Lawson, where you went,
And you're cursing all the business in a bitter discontent;
Well, we grieve to disappoint you, and it makes us sad to hear
That it wasn't cool and shady — and there wasn't plenty beer,
And the loony bullock snorted when you first came into view;
Well, you know it's not so often that he sees a swell like you;
And the roads were hot and dusty, and the plains were burnt and brown,
And no doubt you're better suited drinking lemon squash in town.

Yet, perchance, if you should journey down the very track you went
In a month or two at furthest you would wonder what it meant,
Where the sunbaked earth was gasping like a creature in its pain
You would find the grasses waving like a field of summer grain,
And the miles of thirsty gutters blocked with sand and choked with mud,
You would find them mighty rivers with a turbid, sweeping flood;
For the rain and drought and sunshine make no changes in the street,
In the sullen line of buildings and the ceaseless tramp of feet;
But the bush hath moods and changes, as the seasons rise and fall,
And the men who know the bush land — they are loyal through it all.

But you found the bush was dismal and a land of no delight,
Did you chance to hear a chorus in the shearers' huts at night?
Did they "rise up, William Riley" by the camp-fire's cheery blaze?
Did they rise him as we rose him in the good old droving days?
And the women of the homesteads and the men you chanced to meet —
Were their faces sour and saddened like the "faces in the street",
And the "shy selector children" — were they better now or worse
Than the little city urchins who would greet you with a curse?
Is not such a life much better than the squalid street and square
Where the fallen women flaunt it in the fierce electric glare,
Where the sempstress plies her sewing till her eyes are sore and red
In a filthy, dirty attic toiling on for daily bread?
Did you hear no sweeter voices in the music of the bush
Than the roar of trams and buses, and the war whoop of "the push"?
Did the magpies rouse your slumbers with their carol sweet and strange?
Did you hear the silver chiming of the bellbirds on the range?
But, perchance, the wild birds' music by your senses was despised,
For you say you'll stay in townships till the bush is civilised.
Would you make it a tea garden and on Sundays have a band
Where the "blokes" might take their "donahs", with a "public"
    close at hand?
You had better stick to Sydney and make merry with the "push",
For the bush will never suit you, and you'll never suit the bush.

An Answer to Various Bards

Well, I've waited mighty patient while they all came rolling in,
Mister Lawson, Mister Dyson, and the others of their kin,
With their dreadful, dismal stories of the overlander's camp,
How his fire is always smoky, and his boots are always damp;
And they paint it so terrific it would fill one's soul with gloom,
But you know they're fond of writing about "corpses" and "the tomb".
So, before they curse the bushland they should let their fancy range,
And take something for their livers, and be cheerful for a change.

Now, for instance, Mister Lawson — well, of course, we almost cried
At the sorrowful description how his "little 'Arvie" died.
And we wept in silent sorrow when "His Father's Mate" was slain;
Then he went and killed the father, and we had to weep again.
Ben Duggan and Jack Denver, too, he caused them to expire,
And he went and cooked the gander of Jack Dunn, of Nevertire;
And he spoke in terms prophetic of a revolution's beat,
When the world should hear the clamour of those people in the street;
But the shearer chaps who start it — why, he rounds on them in blame,
And he calls 'em "agitators" who are living on the game.
So, no doubt, the bush is wretched if you judge it by the groan
Of the sad and soulful poet with a graveyard of his own.

But I "over-write" the bushmen! Well, I own without a doubt
That I always see a hero in the "man from furthest out".
I could never contemplate him through an atmosphere of gloom,
And a bushman never struck me as a subject for "the tomb".
If it ain't all "golden sunshine" where the "wattle branches wave",
Well, it ain't all damp and dismal, and it ain't all "lonely grave".
And, of course, there's no denying that the bushman's life is rough,

But a man can easy stand it if he's built of sterling stuff;
Tho' it's seldom that the drover gets a bed of eiderdown,
Yet the man who's born a bushman, he gets mighty sick of town,
For he's jotting down the figures, and he's adding up the bills
While his heart is simply aching for a sight of southern hills.
Then he hears a wool team passing with a rumble and a lurch,
And although the work is pressing yet it brings him off his perch.
For it stirs him like a message from his station friends afar
And he seems to sniff the ranges in the scent of wool and tar;
And it takes him back in fancy, half in laughter, half in tears,
To a sound of other voices and a thought of other years,
When the woolshed rang with bustle from the dawning of the day,
And the shear blades were a-clicking to the cry of "wool away!"
When his face was somewhat browner and his frame was firmer set,
And he feels his flabby muscles with a feeling of regret.
Then the wool team slowly passes and his eyes go sadly back
To the dusty little table and the papers in the rack,
And his thoughts go to the terrace where his sickly children squall,
And he thinks there's something healthy in the bush life after all.

But we'll go no more a-droving in the wind or in the sun,
For our fathers' hearts have failed us and the droving days are done.
There's a nasty dash of danger where the long-horned bullock wheels,
And we like to live in comfort and to get our reg'lar meals.
And to hang about the townships suits us better, you'll agree,
For a job at washing bottles is the job for such as we.
Let us herd into the cities, let us crush and crowd and push
Till we lose the love of roving and we learn to hate the bush;
And we'll turn our aspirations to a city life and beer,
And we'll sneak across to England — it's a nicer place than here;
For there's not much risk of hardship where all comforts are in store,
And the theatres are plenty and the pubs are more and more.

But that ends it, Mister Lawson, and it's time to say good-bye,
We must agree to differ in all friendship, you and I;
And our personal opinions — well, they're scarcely worth a rush,
For there's some that like the city and there's some that like the bush;
And there's no one quite contented, as I've always heard it said,
Except one favoured person, and *he* turned out to be dead.
So we'll work our own salvation with the stoutest hearts we may,
And if fortune only favours we will take the road some day,
And go droving down the river 'neath the sunshine and the stars,
And then we'll come to Sydney and vermilionise the bars.

The Man from Ironbark

It was the man from Ironbark who struck the Sydney town,
   He wandered over street and park, he wandered up and down.
He loitered here, he loitered there, till he was like to drop,
Until at last in sheer despair he sought a barber's shop.
"'Ere! shave my beard and whiskers off, I'll be a man of mark,
I'll go and do the Sydney toff up home in Ironbark."

The barber man was small and flash, as barbers mostly are,
He wore a strike-your-fancy sash, he smoked a huge cigar;
He was a humorist of note and keen at repartee,
He laid the odds and kept a "tote", whatever that may be,
And when he saw our friend arrive, he whispered, "Here's a lark!
Just watch me catch him all alive, this man from Ironbark."

There were some gilded youths that sat along the barber's wall.
Their eyes were dull, their heads were flat, they had no brains at all;

To them the barber passed the wink, his dexter eyelid shut,
"I'll make this bloomin' yokel think his bloomin' throat is cut."
And as he soaped and rubbed it in he made a rude remark:
"I s'pose the flats is pretty green up there in Ironbark."

A grunt was all reply he got; he shaved the bushman's chin,
Then made the water boiling hot and dipped the razor in.
He raised his hand, his brow grew black, he paused awhile to gloat,
Then slashed the red-hot razor-back across his victim's throat;
Upon the newly-shaven skin it made a livid mark —
No doubt it fairly took him in — the man from Ironbark.

He fetched a wild up-country yell might wake the dead to hear,
And though his throat, he knew full well, was cut from ear to ear,
He struggled gamely to his feet, and faced the murd'rous foe:
"You've done for me! you dog, I'm beat! one hit before I go!
I only wish I had a knife, you blessed murdering shark!
But you'll remember all your life the man from Ironbark."

He lifted up his hairy paw, with one tremendous clout
He landed on the barber's jaw, and knocked the barber out.
He set to work with nail and tooth, he made the place a wreck;
He grabbed the nearest gilded youth, and tried to break his neck.
And all the while his throat he held to save his vital spark,
And "Murder! Bloody murder!" yelled the man from Ironbark.

A peelerman who heard the din came in to see the show;
He tried to run the bushman in, but he refused to go.
And when at last the barber spoke, and said "'Twas all in fun —
'Twas just a little harmless joke, a trifle overdone."
"A joke!" he cried, "By George, that's fine; a lively sort of lark;
I'd like to catch that murdering swine some night in Ironbark."

And now while round the shearing floor the list'ning shearers gape,
He tells the story o'er and o'er, and brags of his escape.

"Them barber chaps what keeps a tote, By George, I've had enough,
One tried to cut my bloomin' throat, but thank the Lord it's tough."
And whether he's believed or no, there's one thing to remark,
That flowing beards are all the go way up in Ironbark.

Black Swans

As I lie at rest on a patch of clover
   In the Western Park when the day is done,
I watch as the wild black swans fly over
With their phalanx turned to the sinking sun;
And I hear the clang of their leader crying
To a lagging mate in the rearward flying,
And they fade away in the darkness dying,
Where the stars are mustering one by one.

Oh! ye wild black swans, 'twere a world of wonder
For a while to join in your westward flight,
With the stars above and the dim earth under,
Through the cooling air of the glorious night.
As we swept along on our pinions winging,
We should catch the chime of a church-bell ringing,
Or the distant note of a torrent singing,
Or the far-off flash of a station light.

From the northern lakes with the reeds and rushes,
Where the hills are clothed with a purple haze,
Where the bellbirds chime and the songs of thrushes
Make music sweet in the jungle maze,

They will hold their course to the westward ever,
Till they reach the banks of the old grey river,
Where the waters wash, and the reed beds quiver
In the burning heat of the summer days.

Oh! ye strange wild birds, will ye bear a greeting
To the folk that live in that western land?
Then for every sweep of your pinions beating,
Ye shall bear a wish to the sunburnt band,
To the stalwart men who are stoutly fighting
With the heat and drought and dust storm smiting,
Yet whose life somehow has a strange inviting,
When once to the work they have put their hand.

Facing it yet! Oh, my friend stout-hearted,
What does it matter for rain or shine,
For the hopes deferred and the gain departed?
Nothing could conquer that heart of thine.
And thy health and strength are beyond confessing
As the only joys that are worth possessing.
May the days to come be as rich in blessing
As the days we spent in the auld lang syne.

I would fain go back to the old grey river,
To the old bush days when our hearts were light,
But, alas! those days they have fled for ever,
They are like the swans that have swept from sight.
And I know full well that the strangers' faces
Would meet us now in our dearest places;
For our day is dead and has left no traces
But the thoughts that live in my mind tonight.

There are folk long dead, and our hearts would sicken —
We would grieve for them with a bitter pain,

If the past could live and the dead could quicken,
We then might turn to that life again.
But on lonely nights we would hear them calling,
We should hear their steps on the pathways falling,
We should loathe the life with a hate appalling
In our lonely rides by the ridge and plain.

            *   *   *   *

In the silent park is a scent of clover,
And the distant roar of the town is dead,
And I hear once more as the swans fly over
Their far-off clamour from overhead.
They are flying west by their instinct guided,
And for man likewise is his fate decided,
And griefs apportioned and joys divided
By a mighty power with a purpose dread.

Last Week

Oh, the new chum went to the backblock run,
But he should have gone there last week.
He tramped ten miles with a loaded gun,
But of turkey or duck he saw never a one,
For he should have been there last week,
    They said,
There were flocks of 'em there last week.

He wended his way to a waterfall,
And he should have gone there last week.

He carried a camera, legs and all,
But the day was hot, and the stream was small,
For he should have gone there last week,
    They said,
They drowned a man there last week.

He went for a drive, and he made a start,
Which should have been made last week,
For the old horse died of a broken heart;
So he footed it home and he dragged the cart —
But the horse was all right last week,
    They said,
He trotted a match last week.

So he asked the bushies who came from far
To visit the town last week,
If they'd dine with him, and they said, "Hurrah!"
But there wasn't a drop in the whisky jar —
"You should have been here last week,"
    He said,
"I drank it all up last week!"

A Bush Christening

On the outer Barcoo where the churches are few,
   And men of religion are scanty,
On a road never cross'd 'cept by folk that are lost,
   One Michael Magee had a shanty.

Now this Mike was the dad of a ten-year-old lad,
   Plump, healthy, and stoutly conditioned;
He was strong as the best, but poor Mike had no rest
   For the youngster had never been christened.

And his wife used to cry, "If the darlin' should die
   Saint Peter would not recognise him."
But by luck he survived till a preacher arrived,
   Who agreed straightaway to baptise him.

Now the artful young rogue, while they held their collogue,
   With his ear to the keyhole was listenin',
And he muttered in fright while his features turned white,
   "What the divil and all is this christenin'?"

He was none of your dolts, he had seen them brand colts,
   And it seemed to his small understanding,
If the man in the frock made him one of the flock,
   It must mean something very like branding.

So away with a rush he set off for the bush,
   While the tears in his eyelids they glistened —
"'Tis outrageous," says he, "to brand youngsters like me,
   I'll be dashed if I'll stop to be christened!"

Like a young native dog he ran into a log,
   And his father with language uncivil,

Never heeding the "praste" cried aloud in his haste,
   "Come out and be christened, you divil!"

But he lay there as snug as a bug in a rug,
   And his parents in vain might reprove him,
Till his reverence spoke (he was fond of a joke)
   "I've a notion," says he, "that'll move him."

"Poke a stick up the log, give the spalpeen a prog;
   Poke him aisy — don't hurt him or maim him,
'Tis not long that he'll stand, I've the water at hand,
   As he rushes out this end I'll name him.

"Here he comes, and for shame! ye've forgotten the name —
   Is it Patsy or Michael or Dinnis?"
Here the youngster ran out, and the priest gave a shout —
   "Take your chance, anyhow, wid 'Maginnis'!"

As the howling young cub ran away to the scrub
   Where he knew that pursuit would be risky,
The priest, as he fled, flung a flask at his head
   That was labelled "Maginnis's Whisky!"

And Maginnis Magee has been made a J.P.,
   And the one thing he hates more than sin is
To be asked by the folk who have heard of the joke,
   How he came to be christened "Maginnis"!

The Geebung Polo Club

It was somewhere up the country, in a land of rock and scrub,
That they formed an institution called the Geebung Polo Club.
They were long and wiry natives from the rugged mountainside,
And the horse was never saddled that the Geebungs couldn't ride;
But their style of playing polo was irregular and rash —
They had mighty little science, but a mighty lot of dash:
And they played on mountain ponies that were muscular and strong,
Though their coats were quite unpolished, and their manes and tails
    were long.
And they used to train those ponies wheeling cattle in the scrub:
They were demons, were the members of the Geebung Polo Club.

It was somewhere down the country, in a city's smoke and steam,
That a polo club existed, called the Cuff and Collar Team.
As a social institution 'twas a marvellous success,
For the members were distinguished by exclusiveness and dress.
They had natty little ponies that were nice, and smooth, and sleek,
For their cultivated owners only rode 'em once a week.
So they started up the country in pursuit of sport and fame,
For they meant to show the Geebungs how they ought to play the game;
And they took their valets with them — just to give their boots a rub
Ere they started operations on the Geebung Polo Club.

Now my readers can imagine how the contest ebbed and flowed,
When the Geebung boys got going it was time to clear the road;
And the game was so terrific that ere half the time was gone
A spectator's leg was broken — just from merely looking on.
For they waddied one another till the plain was strewn with dead,
While the score was kept so even that they neither got ahead.
And the Cuff and Collar captain, when he tumbled off to die,
Was the last surviving player — so the game was called a tie.

Then the captain of the Geebungs raised him slowly from the ground,
Though his wounds were mostly mortal, yet he fiercely gazed around;
There was no one to oppose him — all the rest were in a trance,
So he scrambled on his pony for his last expiring chance,
For he meant to make an effort to get victory to his side;
So he struck at goal — and missed it — then he tumbled off and died.

*   *   *   *

By the old Campaspe River, where the breezes shake the grass,
There's a row of little gravestones that the stockmen never pass,
For they bear a crude inscription saying, "Stranger, drop a tear,
For the Cuff and Collar players and the Geebung boys lie here."
And on misty moonlit evenings, while the dingoes howl around,
You can see their shadows flitting down that phantom polo ground;
You can hear the loud collisions as the flying players meet,
And the rattle of the mallets, and the rush of ponies' feet,
Till the terrified spectator rides like blazes to the pub —
He's been haunted by the spectres of the Geebung Polo Club.

The Travelling Post Office

The roving breezes come and go, the reed beds sweep and sway,
    The sleepy river murmurs low, and loiters on its way,
It is the land of lots o' time along the Castlereagh.

*   *   *   *

The old man's son had left the farm, he found it dull and slow,
He drifted to the great North-west where all the rovers go.
"He's gone so long," the old man said, "he's dropped right out of mind,
But if you'd write a line to him I'd take it very kind;
He's shearing here and fencing there, a kind of waif and stray,
He's droving now with Conroy's sheep along the Castlereagh.
The sheep are travelling for the grass, and travelling very slow;
They may be at Mundooran now, or past the Overflow,
Or tramping down the black soil flats across by Waddiwong,
But all those little country towns would send the letter wrong,
The mailman, if he's extra tired, would pass them in his sleep,
It's safest to address the note to 'Care of Conroy's sheep',
For five and twenty thousand head can scarcely go astray,
You write to 'Care of Conroy's sheep along the Castlereagh'."

                    *   *   *   *

By rock and ridge and riverside the western mail has gone,
Across the great Blue Mountain Range to take that letter on.
A moment on the topmost grade while open fire doors glare,
She pauses like a living thing to breathe the mountain air,
Then launches down the other side across the plains away
To bear that note to "Conroy's sheep along the Castlereagh".

And now by coach and mailman's bag it goes from town to town,
And Conroy's Gap and Conroy's Creek have marked it "further down".
Beneath a sky of deepest blue where never cloud abides,
A speck upon the waste of plain the lonely mailman rides.
Where fierce hot winds have set the pine and myall boughs asweep
He hails the shearers passing by for news of Conroy's sheep.
By big lagoons where wildfowl play and crested pigeons flock,
By campfires where the drovers ride around their restless stock,
And past the teamster toiling down to fetch the wool away
My letter chases Conroy's sheep along the Castlereagh.

41

A Bunch of Roses

Roses ruddy and roses white,
  What are the joys that my heart discloses?
Sitting alone in the fading light
Memories come to me here to-night
  With the wonderful scent of the big red roses.

Memories come as the daylight fades
  Down on the hearth where the firelight dozes;
Flicker and flutter the lights and shades,
And I see the face of a queen of maids
  Whose memory comes with the scent of roses.

Visions arise of a scene of mirth,
  And a ballroom belle that superbly poses —
A queenly woman of queenly worth,
And I am the happiest man on earth
  With a single flower from a bunch of roses.

Only her memory lives tonight —
  God in His wisdom her young life closes;
Over her grave may the turf be light,
Cover her coffin with roses white —
  She was always fond of the big white roses.

Such are the visions that fade away —
  Man proposes and God disposes;
Look in the glass and I see to-day
Only an old man, worn and grey,
  Bending his head to a bunch of roses.

How Gilbert Died

There's never a stone at the sleeper's head,
   There's never a fence beside,
And the wandering stock on the grave may tread
   Unnoticed and undenied,
But the smallest child on the Watershed
   Can tell you how Gilbert died.

For he rode at dusk, with his comrade Dunn
   To the hut at the Stockman's Ford,
In the waning light of the sinking sun
   They peered with a fierce accord.
They were outlaws both — and on each man's head
   Was a thousand pounds reward.

They had taken toll of the country round,
   And the troopers came behind
With a black that tracked like a human hound
   In the scrub and the ranges blind:
He could run the trail where a white man's eye
   No sign of a track could find.

He had hunted them out of the One Tree Hill
   And over the Old Man Plain,
But they wheeled their tracks with a wild beast's skill,
   And they made for the range again.
Then away to the hut where their grandsire dwelt,
   They rode with a loosened rein.

And their grandsire gave them a greeting bold:
   "Come in and rest in peace,
No safer place does the country hold —
   With the night pursuit must cease,

And we'll drink success to the roving boys,
    And to hell with the black police."

But they went to death when they entered there,
    In the hut at the Stockman's Ford,
For their grandsire's words were as false as fair —
    They were doomed to the hangman's cord.
He had sold them both to the black police
    For the sake of the big reward.

In the depth of night there are forms that glide
    As stealthy as serpents creep,
And around the hut where the outlaws hide
    They plant in the shadows deep,
And they wait till the first faint flush of dawn
    Shall waken their prey from sleep.

But Gilbert wakes while the night is dark —
    A restless sleeper, aye,
He has heard the sound of a sheepdog's bark,
    And his horse's warning neigh,
And he says to his mate, "There are hawks abroad,
    And it's time that we went away."

Their rifles stood at the stretcher head,
    Their bridles lay to hand,
They wakened the old man out of his bed,
    When they heard the sharp command:
"In the name of the Queen lay down your arms,
    Now, Dunn and Gilbert, stand!"

Then Gilbert reached for his rifle true
    That close at his hand he kept,
He pointed it straight at the voice and drew,
    But never a flash outleapt,

For the water ran from the rifle breach —
   It was drenched while the outlaws slept.

Then he dropped the piece with a bitter oath,
   And he turned to his comrade Dunn:
"We are sold," he said, "we are dead men both,
   But there may be a chance for one;
I'll stop and I'll fight with the pistol here,
   You take to your heels and run."

So Dunn crept out on his hands and knees
   In the dim, half-dawning light,
And he made his way to a patch of trees,
   And vanished among the night,
And the trackers hunted his tracks all day,
   But they never could trace his flight.

But Gilbert walked from the open door
   In a confident style and rash;
He heard at his side the rifles roar,
   And he heard the bullets crash.
But he laughed as he lifted his pistol-hand,
   And he fired at the rifle flash.

Then out of the shadows the troopers aimed
   At his voice and the pistol sound,
With the rifle flashes the darkness flamed,
   He staggered and spun around,
And they riddled his body with rifle balls
   As it lay on the blood-soaked ground.

There's never a stone at the sleeper's head
   There's never a fence beside,

And the wandering stock on the grave may tread
    Unnoticed and undenied,
But the smallest child on the Watershed
    Can tell you how Gilbert died.

The Amateur Rider

*H*im going to ride for us! *Him* — with the pants and the eyeglass and
    all.
Amateur! don't he just look it — it's twenty to one on a fall.
Boss must be gone off his head to be sending our steeplechase crack
Out over fences like these with an object like that on his back.

Ride! Don't tell *me* he can ride. With his pants just as loose as balloons,
How can he sit on his horse? And his spurs like a pair of harpoons;
Ought to be under the Dog Act, he ought, and be kept off the course.
Fall! why, he'd fall off a cart, let alone off a steeplechase horse.

*   *   *   *

Yessir! the 'orse is all ready — I wish you'd have rode him before;
Nothing like knowing your 'orse, sir, and this chap's a terror to bore;
Battleaxe always could pull, and he rushes his fences like fun —
Stands off his jump twenty feet, and then springs like a shot from a gun.

Oh, he can jump 'em all right, sir, you make no mistake, 'e's a toff;
Clouts 'em in earnest, too, sometimes, you mind that he don't clout you off —

Don't seem to mind how he hits 'em, his shins is as hard as a nail,
Sometimes you'll see the fence shake and the splinters fly up
    from the rail.

All you can do is to hold him and just let him jump as he likes,
Give him his head at the fences, and hang on like death if he strikes;
Don't let him run himself out — you can lie third or fourth in the race —
Until you clear the stone wall, and from that you can put on the pace.

Fell at that wall once, he did, and it gave him a regular spread,
Ever since that time he flies it — he'll stop if you pull at his head,
Just let him race — you can trust him — he'll take first-class care
    he don't fall,
And I think that's the lot — but remember, *he must have his head
    at the wall.*

*   *   *   *

Well, he's down safe as far as the start, and he seems to sit on pretty neat,
Only his baggified breeches would ruinate anyone's seat —
They're away — here they come — the first fence, and he's head over heels
    for a crown!
Good for the new chum, he's over, and two of the others are down!

Now for the treble, my hearty — By Jove, he can ride, after all;
Whoop, that's your sort — let him fly them! He hasn't much fear of a fall.
Who in the world would have thought it? And aren't they just
    going a pace?
Little Recruit in the lead there will make it a stoutly run race.

Lord! But they're racing in earnest — and down goes Recruit on his head,
Rolling clean over his boy — it's a miracle if he ain't dead.
Battleaxe, Battleaxe yet! By the Lord, he's got most of 'em beat —
Ho! did you see how he struck, and the swell never moved in his seat?

Second time round, and, by Jingo! he's holding his lead of 'em well;
Hark to him clouting the timber! It don't seem to trouble the swell.

47

Now for the wall — let him rush it. A thirty-foot leap, I declare —
Never a shift in his seat, and he's racing for home like a hare.

What's that that's chasing him — Rataplan — regular demon to stay!
Sit down and ride for your life now! Oh, good, that's the style —
    come away!
Rataplan's certain to beat you, unless you can give him the slip;
Sit down and rub in the whalebone now — give him the spurs
    and the whip!

Battleaxe, Battleaxe, yet — and it's Battleaxe wins for a crown;
Look at him rushing the fences, he wants to bring t'other chap down.
Rataplan never will catch him if only he keeps on his pins;
Now! the last fence! and he's over it! Battleaxe, Battleaxe wins!

*　*　*　*

Well, sir, you rode him just perfect — I knew from the first you could ride.
Some of the chaps said you couldn't, an' I says just like this a' one side:
Mark me, I says, that's a tradesman — the saddle is where he was bred.
Weight! you're all right, sir, and thank you; and them was the words
    that I said.

Saltbush Bill

Now this is the law of the Overland that all in the West obey,
A man must cover with travelling sheep a six-mile stage a day;
But this is the law which the drovers make, right easily understood,
They travel their stage where the grass is bad, but they camp where the
  grass is good;
They camp, and they ravage the squatter's grass till never
  a blade remains,
Then they drift away as the white clouds drift on the edge
  of the saltbush plains,
From camp to camp and from run to run they battle it hand to hand,
For a blade of grass and the right to pass on the track of the Overland.

For this is the law of the Great Stock Routes, 'tis written in white
  and black —
The man that goes with a travelling mob must keep to a half-mile track;
And the drovers keep to a half-mile track on the runs where the grass
  is dead,
But they spread their sheep on a well-grassed run till they go with
  a two-mile spread.
So the squatters hurry the drovers on from dawn till the fall of night,
And the squatters' dogs and the drovers' dogs get mixed in a deadly fight;
Yet the squatters' men, though they hunt the mob, are willing the peace
  to keep,
For the drovers learn how to use their hands when they go with the
  travelling sheep;
But this is the tale of a Jackaroo that came from a foreign strand,
And the fight that he fought with Saltbush Bill, the King of the Overland.

Now Saltbush Bill was a drover tough, as ever the country knew,
He had fought his way on the Great Stock Routes from the sea
  to the Big Barcoo;

He could tell when he came to a friendly run that gave him a chance
        to spread,
And he knew where the hungry owners were that hurried
        his sheep ahead;
He was drifting down in the Eighty drought with a mob that could
        scarcely creep,
(When the kangaroos by the thousands starve, it is rough on the
        travelling sheep.)
And he camped one night at the crossing place on the edge of
        the Wilga run,
"We must manage a feed for them here," he said, "or the half of the mob
        are done!"
So he spread them out when they left the camp wherever
        they liked to go,
Till he grew aware of a Jackaroo with a station hand in tow,
And they set to work on the straggling sheep, and with many
        a stockwhip crack
They forced them in where the grass was dead in the space of the
        half-mile track;
So William prayed that the hand of fate might suddenly strike him blue
But he'd get some grass for his starving sheep in the teeth of that
        Jackaroo.
So he turned and he cursed the Jackaroo, he cursed him alive or dead,
From the soles of his great unwieldy feet to the crown of his ugly head,
With an extra curse on the moke he rode and the cur at his heels
        that ran,
Till the Jackaroo from his horse got down and he went for
        the drover man;
With the station hand for his picker-up, though the sheep ran loose
        the while,
They battled it out on the saltbush plain in the regular prize ring style.

Now, the new chum fought for his honour's sake and the pride of the
        English race,

50

But the drover fought for his daily bread with a smile on his bearded face;
So he shifted ground and he sparred for wind and he made it
    a lengthy mill,
And from time to time as his scouts came in they whispered
    to Saltbush Bill —
"We have spread the sheep with a two-mile spread, and the grass it is
    something grand,
You must stick to him, Bill, for another round for the pride of
    the Overland."

The new chum made it a rushing fight, though never a blow got home,
Till the sun rode high in the cloudless sky and glared on the
    brick-red loam,
Till the sheep drew in to the shelter trees and settled them down to rest,
Then the drover said he would fight no more and he gave his
    opponent best.
So the new chum rode to the homestead straight and he told them
    a story grand
Of the desperate fight that he fought that day with the King of
    the Overland.
And the tale went home to the public schools of the pluck of
    the English swell,
How the drover fought for his very life, but blood in the end must tell.
But the travelling sheep and the Wilga sheep were boxed on
    the Old Man Plain.
'Twas a full week's work ere they drafted out and hunted them off again,
With a week's good grass in their wretched hides, with a curse and a
    stockwhip crack,
They hunted them off on the road once more to starve on
    the half-mile track.
And Saltbush Bill, on the Overland, will many a time recite
How the best day's work that ever he did was the day that he lost
    the fight.

Johnson's Antidote

Down along the Snakebite River, where the overlanders camp,
Where the serpents are in millions, all of the most deadly stamp;
Where the station cook in terror, nearly every time he bakes,
Mixes up among the doughboys half a dozen poison snakes:
Where the wily free selector walks in armour-plated pants,
And defies the stings of scorpions, and the bites of bulldog ants:
Where the adder and the viper tear each other by the throat,
There it was that William Johnson sought his snakebite Antidote.

Johnson was a free selector, and his brain went rather queer,
For the constant sight of serpents filled him with a deadly fear;
So he tramped his free selection, morning, afternoon and night,
Seeking for some great specific that would cure the serpent's bite.
Till King Billy, of the Mooki, chieftain of the flour bag head,
Told him, "Spos'n snake bite pfeller, pfeller mostly drop down dead;
Spos'n snake bite old goanna, then you watch a while you see,
Old goanna cure himself with eating little pfeller tree."
"That's the cure," said William Johnson, "point me out this plant sublime",
But King Billy, feeling lazy, said he'd go another time.
Thus it came to pass that Johnson, having got the tale by rote,
Followed every stray goanna, seeking for the antidote.

*   *   *   *

Loafing once beside the river, while he thought his heart would break,
There he saw a big goanna, fighting with a tiger snake,
In and out they rolled and wriggled, bit each other, heart and soul,
Till the valiant old goanna swallowed his opponent whole.
Breathless, Johnson sat and watched him, saw him struggle up the bank,
Saw him nibbling at the branches of some bushes, green and rank;
Saw him, happy and contented, lick his lips, as off he crept,
While the bulging in his stomach showed where his opponent slept.

Then a cheer of exultation burst aloud from Johnson's throat;
"Luck at last," said he, "I've struck it! 'tis the famous antidote.

"Here it is, the Grand Elixir, greatest blessing ever known,
Twenty thousand men in India die each year of snakes alone.
Think of all the foreign nations, negro, chow, and blackamoor,
Saved from sudden expiration, by my wondrous snakebite cure.
It will bring me fame and fortune! In the happy days to be,
Men of every clime and nation will be round to gaze on me—
Scientific men in thousands, men of mark and men of note,
Rushing down the Mooki River, after Johnson's antidote.
It will cure *delirium tremens*, when the patient's eyeballs stare
At imaginary spiders, snakes which really are not there.
When he thinks he sees them wriggle, when he thinks he sees them bloat,
It will cure him just to think of Johnson's Snakebite Antidote."

Then he rushed to the museum, found a scientific man —
"Trot me out a deadly serpent, just the deadliest you can;
I intend to let him bite me, all the risk I will endure,
Just to prove the sterling value of my wondrous snakebite cure.
Even though an adder bit me, back to life again I'd float;
Snakes are out of date, I tell you, since I've found the antidote."

Said the scientific person, "If you really want to die,
Go ahead — but, if you're doubtful, let your sheepdog have a try.
Get a pair of dogs and try it, let the snake give both a nip;
Give your dog the snakebite mixture, let the other fellow rip;
If he dies and yours survives him, then it proves the thing is good.
Will you fetch your dog and try it?" Johnson rather thought he would.
So he went and fetched his canine, hauled him forward by the throat.
"Stump, old man," says he, "we'll show them we've the genwine antidote."

Both the dogs were duly loaded with the poison gland's contents;
Johnson gave his dog the mixture, then sat down to wait events.
"Mark," he said, "in twenty minutes Stump'll be a-rushing round,

While the other wretched creature lies a corpse upon the ground."
But, alas for William Johnson! ere they'd watched a half-hour's spell
Stumpy was as dead as mutton, t'other dog was live and well.
And the scientific person hurried off with utmost speed,
Tested Johnson's drug and found it was a deadly poison weed;
Half a tumbler killed an emu, half a spoonful killed a goat,
All the snakes on earth were harmless to that awful antidote.

* * * *

Down along the Mooki River, on the overlanders' camp,
Where the serpents are in millions, all of the most deadly stamp,
Wanders, daily, William Johnson, down among those poisonous hordes,
Shooting every stray goanna, calls them "black and yaller frauds".
And King Billy, of the Mooki, cadging for the cast-off coat,
Somehow seems to dodge the subject of the snakebite antidote.

The Daylight is Dying

T he daylight is dying
    Away in the west,
The wild birds are flying
    In silence to rest;
In leafage and frondage
    Where shadows are deep,
They pass to its bondage —
    The kingdom of sleep.
And watched in their sleeping
    By stars in the height,
They rest in your keeping,
    Oh, wonderful night.

When night doth her glories
  Of starshine unfold,
'Tis then that the stories
  Of bushland are told.
Unnumbered I hold them
  In memories bright,
But who could unfold them,
  Or read them aright?
Beyond all denials
  The stars in their glories
The breeze in the myalls
  Are part of these stories.
The waving of grasses,
  The song of the river
That sings as it passes
  For ever and ever,
The hobble chain's rattle,
  The calling of birds,
The lowing of cattle
  Must blend with the words.
Without these, indeed, you
  Would find it ere long,
As though I should read you
  The words of a song
That lamely would linger
  When lacking the rune,
The voice of the singer,
  The lilt of the tune.

But, as one half-hearing
  An old-time refrain,
With memory clearing,
  Recalls it again,
These tales, roughly wrought of

The bush and its ways,
May call back a thought of
The wandering days,
And, blending with each
In the mem'ries that throng,
There haply shall reach
You some echo of song.

The Swagman's Rest

We buried old Bob where the bloodwoods wave
    At the foot of the Eaglehawk;
We fashioned a cross on the old man's grave,
    For fear that his ghost might walk;
We carved his name on a bloodwood tree,
    With the date of his sad decease,
And in place of "Died from effects of spree",
    We wrote, "May he rest in peace".

For Bob was known on the Overland,
    A regular old bush wag,
Tramping along in the dust and sand,
    Humping his well worn swag.
He would camp for days in the river bed,
    And loiter and "fish for whales".
"I'm into the swagman's yard", he said,
    "And I never shall find the rails."

But he found the rails on that summer night
    For a better place — or worse,

As we watched by turns in the flickering light
    With an old black gin for nurse.
The breeze came in with the scent of pine,
    The river sounded clear,
When a change came on, and we saw the sign
    That told us the end was near.

But he spoke in a cultured voice and low —
    "I fancy they've 'sent the route';
I once was an army man, you know,
    Though now I'm a drunken brute;
But bury me out where the bloodwoods wave,
    And if ever you're fairly stuck,
Just take and shovel me out of the grave,
    And, maybe, I'll bring you luck.

"For I've always heard —" here his voice fell weak,
    His strength was well-nigh sped,
He gasped and struggled and tried to speak,
    Then fell in a moment — dead.
Thus ended a wasted life and hard,
    Of energies misapplied —
Old Bob was out of the "swagman's yard"
    And over the Great Divide.

*   *   *   *

The drought came down on the field and flock,
    And never a raindrop fell,
Though the tortured moans of the starving stock
    Might soften a fiend from hell.
And we thought of the hint that the swagman gave
    When he went to the Great Unseen —
We shovelled the skeleton out of the grave
    To see what his hint might mean.

We dug where the cross and the graveposts were,
  We shovelled away the mould,
When sudden a vein of quartz lay bare
  All gleaming with yellow gold.
'Twas a reef with never a fault nor baulk
  That ran from the range's crest,
And the richest mine on the Eaglehawk
  Is known as "The Swagman's Rest".

Under the Shadow of Kiley's Hill

This is the place where they all were bred;
  Some of the rafters are standing still;
Now they are scattered and lost and dead,
Every one from the old nest fled,
  Out of the shadow of Kiley's Hill.

Better it is that they ne'er came back —
  Changes and chances are quickly rung;
Now the old homestead is gone to rack,
Green is the grass on the well-worn track
  Down by the gate where the roses clung.

Gone is the garden they kept with care;
  Left to decay at its own sweet will,
Fruit trees and flower beds eaten bare,
Cattle and sheep where the roses were,
  Under the shadow of Kiley's Hill.

Where are the children that throve and grew
    In the old homestead in days gone by?
One is away on the far Barcoo
Watching his cattle the long year through,
    Watching them starve in the droughts and die.

One in the town where all cares are rife,
    Weary with troubles that cramp and kill,
Fain would be done with the restless strife,
Fain would go back to the old bush life,
    Back to the shadow of Kiley's Hill.

One is away on the roving quest,
    Seeking his share of the golden spoil,
Out in the wastes of the trackless west,
Wandering ever he gives the best
    Of his years and strength to the hopeless toil.

What of the parents? That unkempt mound
    Shows where they slumber united still;
Rough is their grave, but they sleep as sound
Out on the range as on holy ground,
    Under the shadow of Kiley's Hill.

Waltzing Matilda

Carrying a Swag

Oh there once was a swagman camped in the billabongs,
　Under the shade of a Coolibah tree;
And he sang as he looked at the old billy boiling,
　"Who'll come a-waltzing Matilda with me."

　Who'll come a-waltzing Matilda, my darling,
　　Who'll come a-waltzing Matilda with me.
　Waltzing Matilda and leading a water-bag,
　　Who'll come a-waltzing Matilda with me.

Up came the jumbuck to drink at the waterhole,
　Up jumped the swagman and grabbed him in glee;
And he sang as he put him away in his tucker-bag,
　"You'll come a-waltzing Matilda with me."

　Who'll come a-waltzing Matilda, my darling,
　　Who'll come a-waltzing Matilda with me.
　Waltzing Matilda and leading a water-bag,
　　Who'll come a-waltzing Matilda with me.

Up came the squatter a-riding his thoroughbred;
　Up came policemen — one, two, and three.
"Whose is the jumbuck you've got in the tucker-bag?
　You'll come a-waltzing Matilda with we."

　Who'll come a-waltzing Matilda, my darling,
　　Who'll come a-waltzing Matilda with me.
　Waltzing Matilda and leading a water-bag,
　　Who'll come a-waltzing Matilda with me.

Up sprang the swagman and jumped in the waterhole,
　Drowning himself by the Coolibah tree;

And his voice can be heard as it sings in the billabongs,
   "Who'll come a-waltzing Matilda with me?"

Who'll come a-waltzing Matilda, my darling,
   Who'll come a-waltzing Matilda with me.
Waltzing Matilda and leading a water-bag,
   Who'll come a-waltzing Matilda with me.

Brumby's Run

The Aboriginal term for a wild horse is "brumby". At a recent trial in Sydney a Supreme Court Judge, hearing of "brumby horses", asked "Who is Brumby, and where is his run?"

It lies beyond the western pines
   Towards the sinking sun,
And not a survey mark defines
   The bounds of "Brumby's run".

On odds and ends of mountain land
   On tracks of range and rock,
Where no one else can make a stand,
   Old Brumby rears his stock —

A wild, unhandled lot they are
   Of every shape and breed,
They venture out 'neath moon and star
   Along the flats to feed.

But when the dawn makes pink the sky
   And steals along the plain,

The Brumby horses turn and fly
    Towards the hills again.

The traveller by the mountain track
    May hear their hoofbeats pass,
And catch a glimpse of brown and black,
    Dim shadows on the grass.

The eager stock horse pricks his ears
    And lifts his head on high
In wild excitement when he hears
    The Brumby mob go by.

Old Brumby asks no price or fee
    O'er all his wide domains:
The man who yards his stock is free
    To keep them for his pains.

So, off to scour the mountainside
    With eager eyes aglow,
To strongholds where the wild mobs hide
    The gully-rakers go.

A rush of horses through the trees,
    A red shirt making play;
A sound of stockwhips on the breeze,
    They vanish far away!

                    *   *   *   *

Ah, me! before our day is done
    We long with bitter pain
To ride once more on Brumby's run
    And yard his mob again.

Hay and Hell and Booligal

"You come and see me, boys," he said;
   "You'll find a welcome and a bed
  And whisky any time you call;
Although our township hasn't got
The name of quite a lively spot —
  You see, I live in Booligal.

"And people have an awful down
Upon the district and the town —
  Which worse than hell itself they call;
In fact, the saying far and wide
Along the Riverina side
  Is 'Hay and Hell and Booligal'.

"No doubt it suits 'em very well
To say it's worse than Hay or Hell,
  But don't you heed their talk at all;
Of course, there's heat — no one denies —
And sand and dust and stacks of flies,
  And rabbits, too, at Booligal.

"But such a pleasant, quiet place,
You never see a stranger's face —
  They hardly ever care to call;
The drovers mostly pass it by;
They reckon that they'd rather die
  Than spend a night in Booligal.

"The big mosquitoes frighten some —
You'll lie awake to hear 'em hum —
　　And snakes about the township crawl;
But shearers, when they get their cheque,
They never come along and wreck
　　The blessed town of Booligal.

"But down in Hay the shearers come
And fill themselves with fighting rum,
　　And chase blue devils up the wall,
And fight the snaggers every day,
Until there is the deuce to pay —
　　There's none of that in Booligal.

"Of course, there isn't much to see —
The billiard table used to be
　　The great attraction for us all,
Until some careless, drunken curs
Got sleeping on it in their spurs,
　　And ruined it, in Booligal.

"Just now there is a howling drought
That pretty near has starved us out —
　　It never seems to rain at all;
But, if there *should* come any rain,
You couldn't cross the black soil plain —
　　You'd have to stop in Booligal."

＊　　＊　　＊　　＊

"*We'd have to stop!*" With bated breath
We prayed that both in life and death
　　Our fate in other lines might fall:
"Oh, send us to our just reward
In Hay or Hell, but, gracious Lord,
　　Deliver us from Booligal!"

64

Mulga Bill's Bicycle

'Twas Mulga Bill, from Eaglehawk, that caught the cycling craze;
He turned away the good old horse that served him many days;
He dressed himself in cycling clothes, resplendent to be seen;
He hurried off to town and bought a shining new machine;
And as he wheeled it through the door, with air of lordly pride,
The grinning shop assistant said, "Excuse me, can you ride?"

"See here, young man," said Mulga Bill, "from Walgett to the sea,
From Conroy's Gap to Castlereagh, there's none can ride like me.
I'm good all round at everything, as everybody knows,
Although I'm not the one to talk — I *hate* a man that blows.
But riding is my special gift, my chiefest, sole delight;
Just ask a wild duck can it swim, a wildcat can it fight.
There's nothing clothed in hair or hide, or built of flesh or steel,
There's nothing walks or jumps, or runs, on axle, hoof, or wheel,
But what I'll sit, while hide will hold and girth and straps are tight:
I'll ride this here two-wheeled concern right straight away at sight."

'Twas Mulga Bill, from Eaglehawk, that sought his own abode,
That perched above the Dead Man's Creek, beside the mountain road.
He turned the cycle down the hill and mounted for the fray,
But ere he'd gone a dozen yards it bolted clean away.
It left the track, and through the trees, just like a silver streak,
It whistled down the awful slope towards the Dead Man's Creek.

It shaved a stump by half an inch, it dodged a big white box:
The very wallaroos in fright went scrambling up the rocks,
The wombats hiding in their caves dug deeper underground,
As Mulga Bill, as white as chalk, sat tight to every bound.
It struck a stone and gave a spring that cleared a fallen tree,
It raced beside a precipice as close as close could be;

And then as Mulga Bill let out one last despairing shriek
It made a leap of twenty feet into the Dead Man's Creek.

'Twas Mulga Bill, from Eaglehawk, that slowly swam ashore:
He said, "I've had some narrer shaves and lively rides before;
I've rode a wild bull round a yard to win a five-pound bet,
But this was the most awful ride that I've encountered yet.
I'll give that two-wheeled outlaw best; it's shaken all my nerve
To feel it whistle through the air and plunge and buck and swerve.
It's safe at rest in Dead Man's Creek, we'll leave it lying still;
A horse's back is good enough henceforth for Mulga Bill."

With the Cattle

The drought is down on field and flock,
    The river bed is dry;
And we must shift the starving stock
    Before the cattle die.
We muster up with weary hearts
    At breaking of the day,
And turn our heads to foreign parts,
    To take the stock away.
      And it's hunt 'em up and dog 'em,
      And it's get the whip and flog 'em,
For it's weary work is droving when they're
      dying every day;
      By stock routes bare and eaten,
      On dusty roads and beaten,

With half a chance to save their lives we
     take the stock away.

We cannot use the whip for shame
    On beasts that crawl along;
We have to drop the weak and lame,
    And try to save the strong;
The wrath of God is on the track,
    The drought fiend holds his sway,
With blows and cries and stockwhip crack
    We take the stock away.
       As they fall we leave them lying,
        With the crows to watch them dying,
Grim sextons of the Overland that fasten
       on their prey;
       By the fiery dust storm drifting,
       And the mocking mirage shifting,
In heat and drought and hopeless pain we
     take the stock away.

In dull despair the days go by
    With never hope of change,
But every stage we draw more nigh
    Towards the mountain range;
And some may live to climb the pass,
    And reach the great plateau,
And revel in the mountain grass,
    By streamlets fed with snow.
       As the mountain wind is blowing
       It starts the cattle lowing,
And calling to each other down the dusty
       long array;
       And there speaks a grizzled drover:

67

"Well, thank God, the worst is over,
The creatures smell the mountain grass that's
        twenty miles away."

They press towards the mountain grass,
    They look with eager eyes
Along the rugged stony pass,
    That slopes towards the skies;
Their feet may bleed from rocks and stones,
    But though the blood-drop starts,
They struggle on with stifled groans,
    For hope is in their hearts.
        And the cattle that are leading,
        Though their feet are worn and bleeding,
Are breaking to a kind of run — pull up,
        and let them go!
        For the mountain wind is blowing,
        And the mountain grass is growing,
They settle down by running streams ice-cold
        with melted snow.

The days are done of heat and drought
    Upon the stricken plain;
The wind has shifted right about,
    And brought the welcome rain;
The river runs with sullen roar,
    All flecked with yellow foam,
And we must take the road once more,
    To bring the cattle home.
        And it's "Lads! we'll raise a chorus,
        There's a pleasant trip before us."
And the horses bound beneath us as we start
        them down the track;
        And the drovers canter, singing,

Through the sweet green grasses springing,
Towards the far-off mountain land, to bring
    the cattle back.

Are these the beasts we brought away
    That move so lively now?
They scatter off like flying spray
    Across the mountain's brow;
And dashing down the rugged range
    We hear the stockwhip crack,
Good faith, it is a welcome change
    To bring such cattle back.
        And it's "Steady down the lead there!"
        And it's "Let 'em stop and feed there!"
For they're wild as mountain eagles and
        their sides are all afoam;
        But they're settling down already,
        And they'll travel nice and steady,
With cheery call and jest and song we fetch
    the cattle home.

We have to watch them close at night
    For fear they'll make a rush,
And break away in headlong flight
    Across the open bush;
And by the campfire's cheery blaze,
    With mellow voice and strong,
We hear the lonely watchman raise
    The Overlander's song:
        "Oh! it's when we're done with roving,
        With the camping and the droving,
It's homeward down the Bland we'll go,
        and never more we'll roam";
        While the stars shine out above us,

Like the eyes of those who love us —
The eyes of those who watch and wait to greet
    the cattle home.

The plains are all awave with grass,
    The skies are deepest blue;
And leisurely the cattle pass
    And feed the long day through;
But when we sight the station gate,
    We make the stockwhips crack,
A welcome sound to those who wait
    To greet the cattle back:
        And through the twilight falling
        We hear their voices calling,
As the cattle splash across the ford and
        churn it into foam;
        And the children run to meet us,
        And our wives and sweethearts greet us,
Their heroes from the Overland who brought
    the cattle home.

Rio Grande's Last Race

Now this was what Macpherson told
    While waiting in the stand;
A reckless rider, over-bold,
The only man with hands to hold
    The rushing Rio Grande.

He said, "This day I bid goodbye
   To bit and bridle rein,
To ditches deep and fences high,
For I have dreamed a dream, and I
   Shall never ride again.

"I dreamed last night I rode this race
   That I to-day must ride,
And cant'ring down to take my place
I saw full many an old friend's face
   Come stealing to my side.

"Dead men on horses long since dead,
   They clustered on the track;
The champions of the days long fled,
They moved around with noiseless tread —
   Bay, chestnut, brown, and black.

"And one man on a big grey steed
   Rode up and waved his hand;
Said he, 'We help a friend in need,
And we have come to give a lead
   To you and Rio Grande.

" 'For you must give the field the slip,
   So never draw the rein,
But keep him moving with the whip,
And if he falter — set your lip
   And rouse him up again.

" 'But when you reach the big stone wall,
   Put down your bridle hand
And let him sail — he cannot fall —
But don't you interfere at all;
   You trust old Rio Grande.'

"We started, and in front we showed,
    The big horse running free:
Right fearlessly and game he strode,
And by my side those dead men rode
    Whom no one else could see.

"As silently as flies a bird,
    They rode on either hand;
At every fence I plainly heard
The phantom leader give the word,
    'Make room for Rio Grande!'

"I spurred him on to get the lead,
    I chanced full many a fall;
But swifter still each phantom steed
Kept with me, and at racing speed
    We reached the big stone wall.

"And there the phantoms on each side
    Drew in and blocked his leap;
'Make room! make room!' I loudly cried,
But right in front they seemed to ride —
    I cursed them in my sleep.

"He never flinched, he faced it game,
    He struck it with his chest,
And every stone burst out in flame,
And Rio Grande and I became
    As phantoms with the rest.

"And then I woke, and for a space
    All nerveless did I seem;
For I have ridden many a race,
But never one at such a pace
    As in that fearful dream.

"And I am sure as man can be
    That out upon the track,
Those phantoms that men cannot see
Are waiting now to ride with me,
    And I shall not come back.

"For I must ride the dead men's race,
    And follow their command;
'Twere worse than death, the foul disgrace
If I should fear to take my place
    Today on Rio Grande."

He mounted, and a jest he threw,
    With never sign of gloom;
But all who heard the story knew
That Jack Macpherson, brave and true,
    Was going to his doom.

They started, and the big black steed
    Came flashing past the stand;
All single-handed in the lead
He strode along at racing speed,
    The mighty Rio Grande.

But on his ribs the whalebone stung,
    A madness it did seem!
And soon it rose on every tongue
That Jack Macpherson rode among
    The creatures of his dream.

He looked to left and looked to right,
    As though men rode beside;
And Rio Grande, with foam-flecks white,
Raced at his jumps in headlong flight
    And cleared them in his stride.

But when they reached the big stone wall,
    Down went the bridle hand,
And loud we heard Macpherson call,
"Make room, or half the field will fall!
    Make room for Rio Grande!"

"He's down! he's down!" And horse and man
    Lay quiet side by side!
No need the pallid face to scan,
We knew with Rio Grande he ran
    The race the dead men ride.

Pioneers

They came of bold and roving stock that would not fixed abide;
    They were the sons of field and flock since e'er they learned to ride;
We may not hope to see such men in these degenerate years
As those explorers of the bush — the brave old pioneers.

'Twas they who rode the trackless bush in heat and storm and drought;
'Twas they that heard the master-word that called them further out;
'Twas they that followed up the trail the mountain cattle made
And pressed across the mighty range where now their bones are laid.

But now the times are dull and slow, the brave old days are dead
When hardy bushmen started out, and forced their way ahead
By tangled scrub and forests grim towards the unknown west,
And spied the far-off promised land from off the ranges' crest.

Oh! ye, that sleep in lonely graves by far-off ridge and plain,
We drink to you in silence now as Christmas comes again,
The men who fought the wilderness through rough, unsettled years —
The founders of our nation's life, the brave old pioneers.

By the Grey Gulf-water

Far to the Northward there lies a land,
    A wonderful land that the winds blow over,
And none may fathom nor understand
    The charm it holds for the restless rover;
A great grey chaos — a land half made,
    Where endless space is and no life stirreth;
And the soul of a man will recoil afraid
    From the sphinx-like visage that Nature weareth.
But old Dame Nature, though scornful, craves
    Her dole of death and her share of slaughter;
Many indeed are the nameless graves
    Where her victims sleep by the Grey Gulf-water.

Slowly and slowly those grey streams glide,
    Drifting along with a languid motion,
Lapping the reed beds on either side,
    Wending their way to the Northern Ocean.
Grey are the plains where the emus pass
    Silent and slow, with their staid demeanour;
Over the dead men's graves the grass
    Maybe is waving a trifle greener.

Down in the world where men toil and spin
  Dame Nature smiles as man's hand has taught her;
Only the dead men her smiles can win
  In the great lone land by the Grey Gulf-water.

For the strength of man is an insect's strength,
  In the face of that mighty plain and river,
And the life of a man is a moment's length
  To the life of the stream that will run for ever.
And so it cometh they take no part
  In small-world worries; each hardy rover
Rideth abroad and is light of heart,
  With the plains around and the blue sky over.
And up in the heavens the brown lark sings
  The songs that the strange wild land has taught her;
Full of thanksgiving her sweet song rings —
  And I wish I were back by the Grey Gulf-water.

Saltbush Bill's Second Fight

The news came down on the Castlereagh, and went to the world
    at large,
That twenty thousand travelling sheep, with Saltbush Bill in charge,
    Were drifting down from a dried-out run to ravage the Castlereagh;
And the squatters swore when they heard the news, and wished
    they were well away:
For the name and the fame of Saltbush Bill were over the countryside
For the wonderful way that he fed his sheep, and the dodges and
    tricks he tried.

He would lose his way on a main stock route, and stray to the
    squatters' grass;
He would come to a run with the boss away, and swear he had leave
    to pass;
And back of all and behind it all, as well the squatters knew,
If he had to fight, he would fight all day, so long as his sheep got through:
But this is the story of Stingy Smith, the owner of Hard Times Hill,
And the way that he chanced on a fighting man to reckon with
    Saltbush Bill.

*   *   *   *

'Twas Stingy Smith on his stockyard sat, and prayed for an early spring,
When he started at sight of a clean-shaved tramp, who walked with
    jaunty swing;
For a clean-shaved tramp with a jaunty walk a-swinging along the track
Is as rare a thing as a feathered frog on the desolate roads outback.
So the tramp he made for the travellers' hut, and asked could he camp
    the night;
But Stingy Smith had a bright idea, and he said to him, "Can you fight?"
"Why, what's the game?" said the clean-shaved tramp, as he looked at him
    up and down —
"If you want a battle, get off that fence, and I'll kill you for half-a-crown!
But, Boss, you'd better not fight with me, it wouldn't be fair nor right;
I'm Stiffener Joe, from the Rocks Brigade, and I killed a man in a fight:
I served two years for it, fair and square, and now I'm a trampin' back,
To look for a peaceful quiet life away on the outside track —"
"Oh, it's not myself, but a drover chap," said Stingy Smith with glee;
"A bullying fellow, called Saltbush Bill — and you are the man for me.
He's on the road with his hungry sheep, and he's certain to raise a row,
For he's bullied the whole of the Castlereagh till he's got them
    under cow —
Just pick a quarrel and raise a fight, and leather him good and hard,
And I'll take good care that his wretched sheep don't wander
    a half a yard.

77

It's a five-pound job if you belt him well — do anything short of kill,
For there isn't a beak on the Castlereagh will fine you for Saltbush Bill."

"I'll take the job," said the fighting man, "and hot as this cove appears,
He'll stand no chance with a bloke like me, what's lived on
    the game for years;
For he's maybe learnt in a boxing school, and sparred for a round or so,
But I've fought all hands in a ten foot ring each night in a travelling show;
They earnt a pound if they stayed three rounds, and they tried for it
    every night —
In a ten foot ring! Oh, that's the game that teaches a bloke to fight,
For they'd rush and clinch, it was Dublin Rules, and we drew no
    colour line;
And they all tried hard for to earn the pound, but they got no
    pound of mine:
If I saw no chance in the opening round I'd slog at their wind, and wait
Till an opening came — and it *always* came — and I settled 'em,
    sure as fate;
Left on the ribs and right on the jaw — and, when the chance comes,
    make sure!
And it's there a professional bloke like me gets home on an amateur:

"For it's my experience every day, and I make no doubt it's yours,
That a third-class pro is an over-match for the best of the amateurs —"
"Oh, take your swag to the travellers' hut," said Smith, "for you waste
    your breath;
You've a first-class chance, if you lose the fight, of talking your man
    to death.
I'll tell the cook you're to have your grub, and see that you eat your fill,
And come to the scratch all fit and well to leather this Saltbush Bill."

*   *   *   *

'Twas Saltbush Bill, and his travelling sheep were wending their
    weary way

On the Main Stock Route, through the Hard Times Run, on their
    six-milestage a day;
And he strayed a mile from the Main Stock Route, and started
    to feed along,
And, when Stingy Smith came up, Bill said that the Route
    was surveyed wrong;
And he tried to prove that the sheep had rushed and strayed from
    their camp at night,
But the fighting man he kicked Bill's dog, and of course that meant
    a fight:

So they sparred and fought, and they shifted ground and never
    a sound was heard
But the thudding fists on their brawny ribs, and the seconds'
    muttered word,
Till the fighting man shot home his left on the ribs with a mighty clout,
And his right flashed up with a half-arm blow — and Saltbush Bill
    "went out".
He fell face down, and towards the blow; and their hearts with fear
    were filled,
For he lay as still as a fallen tree, and they thought that he must be killed.

So Stingy Smith and the fighting man, they lifted him from the ground,
And sent to home for a brandy flask, and they slowly fetched him round;
But his head was bad, and his jaw was hurt — in fact, he could
    scarcely speak —
So they let him spell till he got his wits, and he camped on the run a week,
While the travelling sheep went here and there, wherever they liked
    to stray,
Till Saltbush Bill was fit once more for the track to the Castlereagh.

                    *   *   *   *

Then Stingy Smith he wrote a note, and gave to the fighting man:
'Twas writ to the boss of the neighbouring run, and thus the missive ran:

"The man with this is a fighting man, one Stiffener Joe by name;
He came near murdering Saltbush Bill, and I found it a costly game:
But it's worth your while to employ the chap, for there isn't the
    slightest doubt
You'll have no trouble from Saltbush Bill while this man hangs about —"
But an answer came by the next week's mail, with news that might
    well appal:
"The man you sent with a note is not a fighting man at all!
He has shaved his beard, and has cut his hair, but I spotted him at a look;
He is Tom Devine, who has worked for years for Saltbush Bill as cook.
Bill coached him up in the fighting yarn, and taught him the tale by rote,
And they shammed to fight, and they got your grass and divided your
    five-pound note.
'Twas a clean take-in, and you'll find it wise — 'twill save you a lot
    of pelf —
When next you're hiring a fighting man, just fight him a round yourself."

*   *   *   *

And the teamsters out on the Castlereagh, when they meet with
    a week of rain,
And the waggon sinks to its axle-tree, deep down in the black soil plain,
When the bullocks wade in a sea of mud, and strain at the load of wool,
And the cattle dogs at the bullocks' heels are biting to make them pull,
When the offside driver flays the team, and curses them while he flogs,
And the air is thick with the language used, and the clamour of men
    and dogs —
The teamsters say, as they pause to rest and moisten each hairy throat,
They wish they could swear like Stingy Smith when he read that
    neighbour's note.

Father Riley's Horse

'Twas the horse thief, Andy Regan, that was hunted like a dog
    By the troopers of the upper Murray side,
They had searched in every gully — they had looked in every log,
    But never sight or track of him they spied,
Till the priest at Kiley's Crossing heard a knocking very late
    And a whisper "Father Riley — come across!"
So his Rev'rence in pyjamas trotted softly to the gate
    And admitted Andy Regan — and a horse!

"Now, it's listen, Father Riley, to the words I've got to say,
    For it's close upon my death I am tonight.
With the troopers hard behind me I've been hiding all the day
    In the gullies keeping close and out of sight.
But they're watching all the ranges till there's not a bird could fly,
    And I'm fairly worn to pieces with the strife,
So I'm taking no more trouble, but I'm going home to die,
    'Tis the only way I see to save my life.

"Yes, I'm making home to mother's, and I'll die o' Tuesday next
    An' be buried on the Thursday — and, of course,
I'm prepared to meet my penance, but with one thing I'm perplexed
    And it's — Father, it's this jewel of a horse!
He was never bought nor paid for, and there's not a man can swear
    To his owner or his breeder, but I know,
That his sire was by Pedantic from the Old Pretender mare
    And his dam was close related to The Roe.

"And there's nothing in the district that can race him for a step,
    He could canter while they're going at their top:
He's the king of all the leppers that was ever seen to lep,
    A five-foot fence — he'd clear it in a hop!
So I'll leave him with you, Father, till the dead shall rise again,

'Tis yourself that knows a good 'un; and, of course,
You can say he's got by Moonlight out of Paddy Murphy's plain
    If you're ever asked the breeding of the horse!

"But it's getting on to daylight and it's time to say goodbye,
    For the stars above the east are growing pale.
And I'm making home to mother — and it's hard for me to die!
    But it's harder still, is keeping out of gaol!
You can ride the old horse over to my grave across the dip
    Where the wattle bloom is waving overhead.
Sure he'll jump them fences easy — you must never raise the whip
    Or he'll rush 'em! — now, goodbye!" and he had fled!

So they buried Andy Regan, and they buried him to rights,
    In the graveyard at the back of Kiley's Hill;
There were five-and-twenty mourners who had five-and-twenty fights
    Till the very boldest fighters had their fill.
There were fifty horses racing from the graveyard to the pub,
    And their riders flogged each other all the while.
And the lashin's of the liquor! And the lavin's of the grub!
    Oh, poor Andy went to rest in proper style.

Then the races came to Kiley's — with a steeplechase and all,
    For the folk were mostly Irish round about,
And it takes an Irish rider to be fearless of a fall,
    They were training morning in and morning out.
But they never started training till the sun was on the course
    For a superstitious story kept 'em back,
That the ghost of Andy Regan on a slashing chestnut horse,
    Had been training by the starlight on the track.

And they read the nominations for the races with surprise
    And amusement at the Father's little joke,
For a novice had been entered for the steeplechasing prize,
    And they found that it was Father Riley's moke!
He was neat enough to gallop, he was strong enough to stay!

But his owner's views of training were immense,
For the Reverend Father Riley used to ride him every day,
   And he never saw a hurdle nor a fence.

And the priest would join the laughter: "Oh," said he, "I put him in,
   For there's five-and-twenty sovereigns to be won.
And the poor would find it useful, if the chestnut chanced to win,
   And he'll maybe win when all is said and done!"
He had called him Faugh-a-ballagh, which is French for "clear the
   course",
   And his colours were a vivid shade of green:
All the Dooleys and O'Donnells were on Father Riley's horse,
   While the Orangemen were backing Mandarin!

It was Hogan, the dog poisoner — aged man and very wise,
   Who was camping in the racecourse with his swag,
And who ventured the opinion, to the township's great surprise,
   That the race would go to Father Riley's nag.
"You can talk about your riders — and the horse has not been schooled,
   And the fences is terrific, and the rest!
When the field is fairly going, then ye'll see ye've all been fooled,
   And the chestnut horse will battle with the best.

"For there's some has got condition, and they think the race is sure,
   And the chestnut horse will fall beneath the weight,
But the hopes of all the helpless, and the prayers of all the poor,
   Will be running by his side to keep him straight.
And it's what's the need of schoolin' or of workin' on the track,
   Whin the saints are there to guide him round the course!
I've prayed him over every fence — I've prayed him out and back!
   And I'll bet my cash on Father Riley's horse!"

               *   *   *   *

Oh, the steeple was a caution! They went tearin' round and round,
   And the fences rang and rattled where they struck.

There was some that cleared the water — there was more fell in and
    drowned,
  Some blamed the men and others blamed the luck!
But the whips were flying freely when the field came into view,
  For the finish down the long green stretch of course,
And in front of all the flyers — jumpin' like a kangaroo,
  Came the rank outsider — Father Riley's horse!

Oh, the shouting and the cheering as he rattled past the post!
  For he left the others standing, in the straight;
And the rider — well they reckoned it was Andy Regan's ghost,
  And it beat 'em how a ghost would draw the weight!
But he weighed in, nine stone seven, then he laughed and disappeared,
  Like a banshee (which is Spanish for an elf),
And old Hogan muttered sagely, "If it wasn't for the beard
  They'd be thinking it was Andy Regan's self!"

And the poor of Kiley's Crossing drank the health at Christmastide
  Of the chestnut and his rider dressed in green.
There was never such a rider, not since Andy Regan died,
  And they wondered who on earth he could have been.
But they settled it among 'em, for the story got about,
  'Mongst the bushmen and the people on the course,
That the Devil had been ordered to let Andy Regan out
  For the steeplechase on Father Riley's horse!

Song of the Pen

Not for the love of women toil we, we of the craft,
  Not for the people's praise.
Only because our Goddess made us her own, and laughed,
  Claiming us all our days.

Claiming our best endeavour, body and heart and brain.
  Given with no reserve.
Niggard is she towards us, granting us little gain,
  Still we are proud to serve.

Not unto us is given choice of the tasks we try —
  Gathering grain or chaff.
One of her favoured servants toils at an epic high,
  One — that a child may laugh.

Yet if we serve her truly in our appointed place,
  Freely she doth accord
Unto her faithful servants always this saving grace;
  Work is its own reward!

85

It's Grand

It's grand to be a squatter
   And sit upon a post,
And watch your little ewes and lambs
   A-giving up the ghost.

It's grand to be a "cockie"
   With wife and kids to keep,
And find an all-wise Providence
   Has mustered all your sheep.

It's grand to be a western man,
   With shovel in your hand,
To dig your little homestead out
   From underneath the sand.

It's grand to be a shearer,
   Along the Darling side,
And pluck the wool from stinking sheep
   That some days since have died.

It's grand to be a rabbit
   And breed till all is blue,
And then to die in heaps because
   There's nothing left to chew.

It's grand to be a Minister
   And travel like a swell,
And tell the central district folk
   To go to — Inverell.

It's grand to be a Socialist
   And lead the bold array
That marches to prosperity
   At seven bob a day.

It's grand to be an unemployed
    And lie in the Domain,
And wake up every second day
    And go to sleep again.

It's grand to borrow English tin
    To pay for wharves and Rocks,
And then to find it isn't in
    The little money-box.

It's grand to be a democrat
    And toady to the mob,
For fear that if you told the truth
    They'd hunt you from your job.

It's grand to be a lot of things
    In this fair southern land,
But if the Lord would send us rain,
    That would, indeed, be grand!

Any Other Time

All of us play our very best game —
    Any other time.
Golf or billiards, it's all the same —
    Any other time.
Lose a match and you always say,
"Just my luck! I was 'off' to-day!
I could have beaten him quite halfway —
    Any other time!"

After a fiver you ought to go —
    Any other time.
Every man that you ask says "Oh,
    Any *other* time.
Lend you a fiver! I'd lend you two,
But I'm overdrawn and my bills are due,
Wish you'd ask me — now, mind you do —
    Any other time!"

Fellows will ask you out to dine —
    Any other time.
"Not tonight, for we're twenty-nine —
    Any other time.
Not tomorrow, for cook's on strike —
Not next day, I'll be out on the bike —
Just drop in whenever you like —
    Any other time!"

Seasick passengers like the sea —
    Any other time.
"Something . . . I ate . . . disagreed . . . with me!
    Any other time
Ocean-trav'lling is . . . simply bliss,
Must be my . . . liver . . . has gone amiss . . .
Why, I would laugh . . . at a sea . . . like this —
    Any other time."

Most of us mean to be better men —
    Any other time:
Regular upright characters then —
    Any other time.
Yet somehow as the years go by
Still we gamble and drink and lie,
When it comes to the last we'll want to die —
    Any other time!

In the Stable

W hat! You don't like him; well, maybe — we all have our fancies,
    of course:
Brumby to look at you reckon? Well, no: he's a thoroughbred horse;
Sired by a son of old Panic — look at his ears and his head —
Lop-eared and Roman-nosed, ain't he? — well, that's how
    the Panics are bred.
Gluttonous, ugly and lazy, rough as a tip-cart to ride,
Yet if you offered a sovereign apiece for the hairs on his hide
That wouldn't buy him, nor twice that; while I've a pound to the good,
This here old stager stays by me and lives like a thoroughbred should:
Hunt him away from his bedding, and sit yourself down by the wall,
Till you hear how the old fellow saved me from Gilbert, O'Maley and Hall.

*   *   *   *

Gilbert and Hall and O'Maley, back in the bushranging days,
Made themselves kings of the district — ruled it in old-fashioned ways —
Robbing the coach and the escort, stealing our horses at night,
Calling sometimes at the homesteads and giving the women a fright:
Came to the station one morning — and why they did this
    no one knows —
Took a brood mare from the paddock — wanting some fun, I suppose —
Fastened a bucket beneath her, hung by a strap round her flank,
Then turned her loose in the timber back of the seven-mile tank.

Go! She went mad! She went tearing and screaming with fear
    through the trees,
While the curst bucket beneath her was banging her flanks
    and her knees.
Bucking and racing and screaming she ran to the back of the run,
Killed herself there in a gully; by God, but they paid for their fun!
Paid for it dear, for the black boys found tracks, and the bucket, and all,
And I swore that I'd live to get even with Gilbert, O'Maley and Hall.

89

Day after day then I chased them — 'course they had friends on the sly,
Friends who were willing to sell them to those who were willing to buy.
Early one morning we found them in camp at the Cockatoo Farm
One of us shot at O'Maley and wounded him under the arm:
Ran them for miles in the ranges, till Hall, with his horse fairly beat,
Took to the rocks and we lost him — the others made good their retreat.
It was war to the knife then, I tell you, and once, on the door of my shed,
They nailed up a notice that offered a hundred reward for my head!

Then we heard they were gone from the district, they stuck up a coach
    in the West,
And I rode by myself in the paddocks, taking a bit of a rest,
Riding this colt as a youngster — awkward, half-broken and shy,
He wheeled round one day on a sudden; I looked, but I couldn't see why,
But I soon found out why, for before me, the hillside rose up like a wall,
And there on the top with their rifles were Gilbert, O'Maley and Hall!

'Twas a good three-mile run to the homestead — bad going, with plenty
    of trees —
So I gathered the youngster together, and gripped at his ribs
    with my knees.
'Twas a mighty poor chance to escape them! It puts a man's nerve
    to the test
On a half-broken colt to be hunted by the best mounted men in the West.
But the half-broken colt was a racehorse! He lay down to work with a will,
Flashed through the scrub like a clean-skin — by Heavens we *flew*
    down the hill!
Over a twenty-foot gully he swept with the spring of a deer
And they fired as we jumped, but they missed me — a bullet sang
    close to my ear —
And the jump gained us ground, for they shirked it: but I saw as we
    raced through the gap
That the rails at the homestead were fastened — I was caught like a rat
    in a trap.

90

Fenced with barbed wire was the paddock — barbed wire that would cut
  like a knife —
How was a youngster to clear it that never had jumped in his life?

Bang went a rifle behind me — the colt gave a spring, he was hit;
Straight at the sliprails I rode him — I felt him take hold of the bit;
Never a foot to the right or the left did he swerve in his stride,
Awkward and frightened, but honest, the sort it's a pleasure to ride!
Straight at the rails, where they'd fastened barbed wire on the top
  of the post,
Rose like a stag and went over, with hardly a scratch at the most;
Into the homestead I darted, and snatched down my gun from the wall,
And I tell you I made them step lively, Gilbert, O'Maley and Hall!

Yes! There's the mark of the bullet — he's got it inside of him yet
Mixed up somehow with his victuals, but bless you he don't seem to fret!
Gluttonous, ugly, and lazy — eats any thing he can bite;
Now, let us shut up the stable, and bid the old fellow goodnight:
Ah! We can't breed 'em, the sort that were bred when we old 'uns
  were young.
Yes, I was saying, these bushrangers, none of 'em lived to be hung,
Gilbert was shot by the troopers, Hall was betrayed by his friend,
Campbell disposed of O'Maley, bringing the lot to an end.

But you can talk about riding — I've ridden a lot in the past —
Wait till there's rifles behind you, you'll know what it means to go fast!
I've steeplechased, raced, and "run horses", but I think the most
  dashing of all
Was the ride when the old fellow saved me from Gilbert, O'Maley
  and Hall!

The Old Australian Ways

The London lights are far abeam
    Behind a bank of cloud,
Along the shore the gas lights gleam,
    The gale is piping loud;
And down the Channel, groping blind,
    We drive her through the haze
Towards the land we left behind —
The good old land of "never mind",
    And old Australian ways.

The narrow ways of English folk
    Are not for such as we;
They bear the long-accustomed yoke
    Of staid conservancy:
But all our roads are new and strange
    And through our blood there runs
The vagabonding love of change
That drove us westward of the range
    And westward of the suns.

The city folk go to and fro
    Behind a prison's bars,
They never feel the breezes blow
    And never see the stars;
They never hear in blossomed trees
    The music low and sweet
Of wild birds making melodies,
Nor catch the little laughing breeze
    That whispers in the wheat.

Our fathers came of roving stock
    That could not fixed abide:

And we have followed field and flock
    Since e'er we learnt to ride;
By miner's camp and shearing shed,
    In land of heat and drought,
We followed where our fortunes led,
With fortune always on ahead
    And always further out.

The wind is in the barley grass,
    The wattles are in bloom;
The breezes greet us as they pass
    With honey-sweet perfume;
The parakeets go screaming by
    With flash of golden wing,
And from the swamp the wild ducks cry
Their long-drawn note of revelry,
    Rejoicing at the spring.

So throw the weary pen aside
    And let the papers rest,
For we must saddle up and ride
    Towards the blue hill's breast;
And we must travel far and fast
    Across their rugged maze,
To find the Spring of Youth at last,
And call back from the buried past
    The old Australian ways.

When Clancy took the drover's track
    In years of long ago,
He drifted to the outer back
    Beyond the Overflow;
By rolling plain and rocky shelf,
    With stockwhip in his hand,
He reached at last, oh lucky elf,

The Town of Come-and-Help-Yourself
In Rough-and-Ready Land.

And if it be that you would know
The tracks he used to ride,
Then you must saddle up and go
Beyond the Queensland side —
Beyond the reach of rule or law,
To ride the long day through,
In Nature's homestead — filled with awe:
You then might see what Clancy saw
And know what Clancy knew.

Song of the Wheat

We have sung the song of the droving days,
Of the march of the travelling sheep;
By silent stages and lonely ways
Thin, white battalions creep.
But the man who now by the land would thrive
Must his spurs to a ploughshare beat.
Is there ever a man in the world alive
To sing the song of the Wheat!

It's west by south of the Great Divide
The grim grey plains run out,
Where the old flock masters lived and died
In a ceaseless fight with drought.
Weary with waiting and hope deferred
They were ready to own defeat,

Till at last they heard the master-word
 And the master-word was Wheat.

Yarran and Myall and Box and Pine —
 'Twas axe and fire for all;
They scarce could tarry to blaze the line
 Or wait for the trees to fall,
Ere the team was yoked and the gates flung wide,
 And the dust of the horses' feet
Rose up like a pillar of smoke to guide
 The wonderful march of Wheat.

Furrow by furrow, and fold by fold,
 The soil is turned on the plain;
Better than silver and better than gold
 Is the surface-mine of the grain.
Better than cattle and better than sheep
 In the fight with the drought and heat.
For a streak of stubbornness wide and deep
 Lies hid in a grain of Wheat.

When the stock is swept by the hand of fate,
 Deep down in his bed of clay
The brave brown Wheat will lie and wait
 For the resurrection day:
Lie hid while the whole world thinks him dead;
 But the spring rain, soft and sweet,
Will over the steaming paddocks spread
 The first green flush of the Wheat.

Green and amber and gold it grows
 When the sun sinks late in the West
And the breeze sweeps over the rippling rows
 Where the quail and the skylark nest.
Mountain or river or shining star,

There's never a sight can beat —
Away to the skyline stretching far —
    A sea of the ripening Wheat.

When the burning harvest sun sinks low,
    And the shadows stretch on the plain,
The roaring strippers come and go
    Like ships on a sea of grain;
Till the lurching, groaning waggons bear
    Their tale of the load complete.
Of the world's great work he has done his share
    Who has gathered a crop of wheat.

Princes and Potentates and Czars,
    They travel in regal state,
But old King Wheat has a thousand cars
    For his trip to the water-gate;
And his thousand steamships breast the tide
    And plough thro' the wind and sleet
To the lands where the teeming millions bide
    That say, "Thank God for Wheat!"

"We're All Australians Now"

Australia takes her pen in hand,
　　To write a line to you,
To let you fellows understand,
　　How proud we are of you.

From shearing shed and cattle run,
　　From Broome to Hobson's Bay,
Each native-born Australian son,
　　Stands straighter up today.

The man who used to "hump his drum",
　　On far-out Queensland runs,
Is fighting side by side with some
　　Tasmanian farmer's sons.

The fisher-boys dropped sail and oar
　　To grimly stand the test,
Along that storm-swept Turkish shore,
　　With miners from the west.

The old state jealousies of yore
　　Are dead as Pharaoh's sow,
We're not State children any more
　　We're all Australians now!

Our six-starred flag that used to fly,
　　Half-shyly to the breeze,
Unknown where older nations ply
　　Their trade on foreign seas,

Flies out to meet the morning blue
    With Vict'ry at the prow;
For that's the flag the *Sydney* flew,
    The wide seas know it now!

The mettle that a race can show,
    Is proved with shot and steel,
And now we know what nations know
    And feel what nations feel.

The honoured graves beneath the crest
    Of Gaba Tepe hill,
May hold our bravest and our best,
    But we have brave men still.

With all our petty quarrels done,
    Dissensions overthrown,
We have, through what you boys have done,
    A history of our own.

Our old world diff'rences are dead,
    Like weeds beneath the plough,
For English, Scotch, and Irish-bred,
    They're all Australians now!

So now we'll toast the Third Brigade,
    That led Australia's van,
For never shall their glory fade
    In minds Australian.

Fight on, fight on, unflinchingly,
    Till right and justice reign.
Fight on, fight on, till Victory
    Shall send you home again.

And with Australia's flag shall fly
A spray of wattle bough,
To symbolise our unity,
We're all Australians now.

The Old Tin Hat

In the good old days when the Army's ways were simple and unrefined,
With a stock to keep up their chins in front, and a pigtail down behind,
When the only light in the barracks at night was a candle of grease or
fat,
When they put the extinguisher on the light, they called it the Old Tin
Hat.

Now, a very great man is the C. in C., for he is the whole of the show —
The reins and the whip and the driver's hand that maketh the team to
go —
But the road he goes is a lonely road, with ever a choice to make,
When he comes to a place where the roads divide, which one is the road
to take.
For there's one road right, and there's one road wrong, uphill, or over the
flat,
And one road leads to the Temple of Fame, and one to the Old Tin Hat.

And a very great man is the man who holds an Army Corps command,
For he hurries his regiments here and there as the C. in C. has planned.
By day he travels about in state and stirreth them up to rights,
He toileth early and toileth late, and sitteth up half the nights;

But the evening comes when the candle throws twin shadows upon the mat,
And one of the shadows is like a wreath, and one like an Old Tin Hat.

And a very proud man is the Brigadier at the sound of the stately tread
Of his big battalions marching on, as he rides with his staff ahead.
There's never a band to play them out, and the bugle's note is still,
But he hears two tunes in the gentle breeze that blows from over the hill.
And one is a tune in a stirring key, and the other is faint and flat,
For one is the tune of "My new C.B." and the other, "My Old Tin Hat".

And the Colonel heading his regiment is life and soul of the show,
It's "Column of Route", "Form troops", "Extend", and into the fight they go;
He does not duck when the air is full of the "wail of the whimpering lead",
He does not scout for the deep dugout when the 'planes are overhead;
He fears not hog, nor devil, nor dog, and he'd scrap with a mountain cat,
But he goeth in fear of the Brigadier, and in fear of the Old Tin Hat.

Index of Titles

101

Index of First Lines